the complete indonesian cookbook

Agnes de Keijzer Brackman • Cathay Brackman

mc Marshall Cavendish
Cuisine

First published 1970
Reprinted as The Art of Indonesian Cooking (1974), Cook Indonesian (1982, 1991, 1994, 2005)
This edition © 2009 by Marshall Cavendish International (Asia) Private Limited

Cover design by Bernard Go Kwang Meng
Food photographs by Joshua Tan; authors' photograph by Sue Brisk

Published by Marshall Cavendish Cuisine
An imprint of Marshall Cavendish International
1 New Industrial Road, Singapore 536196

Other Marshall Cavendish Offices:
Marshall Cavendish Ltd. 5th Floor, 32-38 Saffron Hill, London EC1N 8FH, UK • Marshall Cavendish Corporation. 99 White Plains Road, Tarrytown NY 10591-9001, USA • Marshall Cavendish International (Thailand) Co Ltd. 253 Asoke, 12th Flr, Sukhumvit 21 Road, Klongtoey Nua, Wattana, Bangkok 10110, Thailand • Marshall Cavendish (Malaysia) Sdn Bhd, Times Subang, Lot 46, Subang Hi-Tech Industrial Park, Batu Tiga, 40000 Shah Alam, Selangor Darul Ehsan, Malaysia

Marshall Cavendish is a trademark of Times Publishing Limited

National Library Board Singapore Cataloguing in Publication Data

Brackman, Agnes de Keijzer.
The complete Indonesian cookbook / Agnes de Keijzer Brackman, Cathay Brackman. –
Singapore : Marshall Cavendish Cuisine, 2009.
p. cm.
ISBN-13 : 978-981-261-784-2
ISBN-10 : 981-261-784-1

1. Cookery, Indonesian. I. Brackman, Cathay. II. Title.

TX724.5.I5
641.59598 -- dc22   OCN304076478

Printed in Singapore by Times Printers Pte Ltd

Dedication

*As we finish these pages, our thoughts
are with the victims of the tsunami.
December 26, 2004.*

Acknowledgements

The publisher wishes to thank to all those
who have contributed to the production of
The Complete Indonesian Cookbook, especially
Blue Canopy and **Royal Selangor** for the loan
and use of their tableware.

$\mathcal{C}$ontents

Preface

Eating and sharing Indonesian food has always been an important part of my life. I was born in Surinam, formerly called Dutch Guiana, in South America. Surinam's population is 15 per cent Indonesian, a very large cultural influence. Actually, this tiny nation has a very diverse population, including Indonesian, Chinese, Dutch, Maroon, Amerindian, East Indian and Creole peoples.

Surinam's food reveals its influences — African peanuts, East Indian curries and *roti* (flat breads), Chinese food with its salty soy, Indonesian with its sweet soy, and the Dutch influence of split pea soup (but in Surinam, inexplicably, served over soft-boiled rice).

A large crop in Surinam is rice. When the *padi* was ready for harvesting, the rice plantations would hold big *selamatans* with Indonesian food and *gamelan* music. My brothers, sister and I would visit our Javanese friends to join the celebration and fill ourselves with delicious food. As such, I grew up knowing how Indonesian food tasted but not how to cook it. I knew some of the language and the customs but not the country. So, when I joined the KNIL (Royal Netherlands Indies Army) during World War II, I was looking forward to finally visiting "The Indies". In August 1945, right after the Japanese surrendered, I was at Camp Columbia in Brisbane, Australia. My group was charged with registering and repatriating the POWs in the Indies. I left for Batavia, now Jakarta, on a C47 (DAKOTA) and island hopped to Java via Merauke, Biak, Morotai, Balikpapan. There, I was assigned to Camp Tjideng on Laan Trivelli, Batavia, where 10,000 women and children were interred. Today, I still am in awe at the courage and strength of the people who managed to survive under those deplorable circumstances.

Three years later, I met my husband, Arnold (Brack). He was a journalist who had covered the War Crimes trials in Tokyo and was assigned by the United Press to cover what was then called the "Indo-Dutch situation". I ask you, what is more normal in wartime than for a North American and a South American to meet in Java and get married?

It was a very exciting time in Batavia; the city was filled with foreign correspondents and photographers covering the transfer of sovereignty from the Netherlands. Being married to a journalist had many advantages. I met President Sukarno, the Sultan of Djokja, Sutan Shahrir, vice president Hatta and many, many others. Brack and I were guests at the first reception after Indonesian independence in 1950.

When my husband was reassigned, and he and I moved to New York City, we desperately missed the food. I had no idea how to cook anything but *nasi goreng* and even if I did know how to cook, finding ingredients in America was impossible back then; American tastes were not very adventurous. My husband and I made do with eating at Chinese and Indian restaurants but the unique tastes of Indonesia were not possible for us to enjoy.

When we returned to Indonesia a year and a half later, I was ready to learn how to cook the food we loved and, oh, so missed. We were very fortunate to get a small house in Kebajoran Baruh, just outside of Jakarta. We were the only foreigners living there and our cook, Mama Masiem, taught me how to cook Indonesian — over a two-burner kerosene stove and a small portable stove. So, I learned the basics of Indonesian cooking in a kitchen equipped with only the bare basics. Now when I cook, I use rice cookers, electric grinders, food processors and mixers. Nevertheless, old habits are hard to stop and I still prefer to grind my spices by hand on my old stone mortar and pestle, called *batu lesong* or *ulekaw* by the locals, and I often forgo the rice cooker for my ancient rice pot.

Today, I take a lot of shortcuts when I cook. I can buy grilled *tempe* (fermented soy bean cakes), already sliced; all I do is fry onions and *kecap* (sweet soy sauce) and mix them together. I believe that no well-equipped kitchen should be without at least one jar of good *sambal badjak* and *sambal oelek*, both now easily obtainable in even the U.S.

So much has changed in the last few decades. Twenty years ago, the average American had never heard of tamarind or lemon grass. Today, we have an array of Thai, Malay, Chinese, Japanese, Indian and Indonesian spices, dipping sauces, soy sauces, fruits and vegetables. I can easily purchase tofu in different flavours — from plain (with the options of extra-soft, soft, firm, and extra firm) to strawberry- and garlic-flavoured. We have so many choices! In my local market, I have Mongolian hot oil, wasabi, brinjal (Asian aubergine/eggplant), relishes, etc. You name it, it's available.

I no longer grate my own coconuts to make *santan*. Coconut milk comes in cans and grated coconut comes in a bag from the frozen section of the supermarket. While I can buy fresh cassava (tapioca), I can also buy it already peeled in the frozen section of my supermarket.

I no longer fry my own shallots, onions and garlic to sprinkle over *nasi kuning*; Thailand is a great exporter of these items (speaking of shallots, when I first arrived in the U.S., shallots could only be obtained through a single mail-order source!). This past autumn, I took a drive to look at the lovely fall foliage in upstate New York and in a small Hudson Valley shop, I found one of my favourite condiments — Lingham sauce from Malaysia. Incidentally, Lingham sauce comes in more than a dozen different varieties and will complement Western foods such as fried chicken or fish.

Now, fusion cooking is served in the finest restaurants because many of America's great chefs mix European styles and flavours with Asian influences, and almost every supermarket in my small area of Connecticut offers freshly made sushi. With the global economy, we can get most ingredients from durian to lychees (litchis) and rambutans. Alas, the fruit that has not yet made a successful transfer to America is the fabulous and delicate mangosteen (although I did find it in Harrods, London, one Christmas). Fruits and vegetables cannot really be considered seasonal — we get virtually everything from all over the world at any time of the year.

For this edition, several recipes have been added. These recipes are what my daughter, Cathay, deems "home cooking". Indeed, I consider that the way I cook is simply my version of home cooking. When my daughter first went to college, she was exposed for the first time to her roommates' home cooking — shepherd's pie, kielbasa, lasagna; these dishes were never served when she was growing up. Cathay tells me that she recently contacted an old roommate who told her that she still was making stir-fry the way that Cathay had taught her in college.

I would advise that the first time you cook Indonesian, that you follow the recipe exactly since you may not be familiar with the tastes. The next time you cook the dish, however, you will know what flavours you would like to enhance. You might want to add more thin or light soy to diminish the sweetness or you might want to add more red chillies (hot peppers). You would then tailor the basic recipe to your own tastes. Because recipes are really just starting points, they are loose road maps, and the recipes contained in this book are my own, personal road maps. When my daughter cooks the same recipe, she adds and deletes as she pleases. Also, I don't believe that you just get recipes from cookbooks. For me, they open the worlds of other cultures and enrich our lives. I love reading recipes even when I don't intend to use them.

So, go to the store and get a few cans of coconuts milk, a container of fried shallots and/or garlic. Start putting them together and you will discover that Indonesian cooking is just home cooking from another culture. The recipe doesn't have to be intricate. For instance, when I was growing up in Surinam, I had a favourite *petjil*, which was simply cooked, cut long beans and water convolvulus or spinach (*kangkung*), a green vegetable similar to watercress; the *petjil* was smothered in a hot peanut sauce and served in a banana-leaf pouch. Another simple dish I make at the end of the summer growing season involves taking the leaves of my pepper plants and stir-frying them quickly with a bit of oil, chopped garlic, and a touch of dried prawn (shrimp) paste (*terasi*); the simple taste is outstanding. As for my daughter, nothing can really top a dish of plain, white rice and *sambal goreng tempe*, or spicy fermented soy bean cakes.

I would like to acknowledge many of my friends who survived my cooking and who I remember well — the late former Singapore President and Mrs. Wee Kim Wee; former Indonesian Vice President and Mrs. Hatta; Mrs. Sardjan (who knew I loved *petjil* and would often send me a large plateful; a gesture that I returned with homemade potato salad); General and Mrs. Simatupang; Sutan Shahrir in Tjawi; the Sastrosatomo brothers, Badio and Darpo; Anak Agung and Vera; Muter; Rosihan Anwar; Lily and Sjafruddin Prawiranegara; Ali and Miriam Budiardjo; Mariah Ulfah Santoso; Adam Malik; Mr. and Mrs. Mohammad Natsire; Mr. and Mrs. Mohammad Roem; Arnold Mononutu (the first Indonesian ambassador to Beijing and we were there at the ship to wish him bon voyage); Pak Sakun and Masiem; Wagira; ma Klewon; ma Samigoe and my mother, Betsy Wong deKeyzer. I have included a recipe for homemade *tempe* (fermented soy bean cakes) that I got from Mrs. Josuf Ronodipuro (thanks, Titi) which my daughter insists results in "real *tempe*". If I have failed to mention some friends — *ma'af*.

On September 17, 2005, it will be exactly 60 years since I first arrived in Batavia (now Indonesia). I am writing this just before Christmas 2004. Last night, my daughter and I sat in front of the fireplace making dinner in our Mongolian hot pot. (This meal goes by many names. In Singapore, if I recall correctly, it is called a "steamboat" dinner; in Japan, it is *shabu shabu*.) I filled the bottom of our Mongolian brazier with burning charcoal and I had ready a very rich chicken broth, which I then poured into the pot. In preparation, I had sliced some beef very, very thinly. I also had sliced chicken breasts, shelled prawns (shrimps), mung bean thread (glass or transparent noodles), watercress and a package of firm tofu. Cathay and I had our individual utensils and we picked morsels of food and cooked it in the broth. On the side, we had a variety of dipping sauces and as we cook and ate, the broth got richer and richer until, at the end, we had a wonderfully flavourful broth.

As we sat by the fire and made our dinner, I reminisced about my days in Indonesia and the wonderful and lucky life I have had. As never before, I realised how so much of my life has centred on food and cooking, and the community of eating together. From my early days in Surinam and the *selamatans* when the rice was harvested to first arriving in Indonesia after World War II to Kebajoran and the journalists sitting at my table to our Indonesian and Asian friends visiting my husband and I in New York to a quiet evening with my daughter in Connecticut.

Agnes de Keijzer Brackman
Brookfield Center, Connecticut

A Quick Reference

Coconut milk This ingredient is absolutely indispensable not only in Indonesian cooking, but virtually in all forms of South Asian cooking except for the Chinese. When I first wrote this cookbook, you had to buy a whole coconut and prepare it yourself. Now, you can buy excellent coconut milk in cans but I've included the old way, just in case you want to try it.

Contrary to popular belief in the West, the refreshing, colourless liquid inside the coconut is not coconut milk. The preparation of coconut milk is not difficult, fortunately.

a) Purchase a fresh coconut and pierce one of the nut's eyes at the top. Use a sharp object such as a plain, down-to-earth screwdriver. Drain the liquid from the coconut and serve as a drink. Children love it.

b) Now, place the coconut in an oven, raise the temperature to 205°C/400°F and heat for about 20 minutes. Leave the coconut to cool, then break it open with a hammer.

c) Remove the flesh from the shell with a dull paring knife. Remove the brown outer skin from the flesh with a potato peeler.

d) Wash and grate the coconut flesh. Add warm water as the recipe requires. For example, if a recipe calls for "½ cup coconut milk from ½ coconut", simply add ½ cup (125 ml) of warm water to 2 cups of grated coconut. One coconut yields 4 cups of grated coconut.

e) After the coconut 'milk' is cooled, strain through cheesecloth. (Squeeze grated coconut until all the milk is extracted.) The milk is now ready for use.

Tamarind juice To prepare tamarind juice, place an amount of tamarind pulp about the size of a domino in 2 tablespoons of lukewarm water, stir and stand for an hour. This is more than enough for all recipes requiring tamarind juice. Blocks of tamarind pulp are easily bought in the U.S. but take care that the tamarind is not sweet tamarind.

Bean sprouts To make fresh bean sprouts, place ½ cup mung or green beans (available in any Chinatown) in a dish. Add enough tepid water to barely cover them. Cover dish and place in a dark cupboard. Check daily, add additional water to keep beans moist (but do not saturate). Beans should be ready in 3–4 days. You can buy bean sprouts in almost any market but take care to wash thoroughly.

Chicken Chicken dishes may be made a day before they are to be served and placed in the refrigerator in a covered dish.

Fish and shellfish To save time, clean fish and shellfish in advance, salt lightly and place in refrigerator until needed.

Cabbage and string bean dishes These improve in flavour if made a day in advance of serving and kept refrigerated.

Krupuk* and *rempeyeh Both can be fried the day before, thoroughly cooled and kept in an airtight container until needed. They make excellent cocktail titbits.

Relishes Relishes and pickled dishes may be made several days in advance and stored for considerable periods in mason jars, tightly sealed and refrigerated.

Grated coconut Coconuts may be grated a week or more in advance and placed in either a Pyrex dish or plastic freezing bag and kept in a deep freezer. Remove from the freezer several hours before needed.

Keeping food warm Dishes prepared the day before may be heated without burning by keeping the range at low heat while placing the dishes in the oven compartment. Dishes may be left in the oven for an hour or more while preparing the rice.

Rice For perfect rice, each grain separate and distinct, rinse American rice twice before cooking and Asian-grown varieties several times. This washes away the small particles acquired during the milling process. If you like rice, be sure to buy a rice cooker. It will make your life so much easier.

Satay Wrap ends of bamboo *satay* skewers with aluminium foil to prevent them from burning during a barbecue, Western style. Alternatively, soak them in water and drain before use. An electric blender (processor) is a wonderful coconut grater and can also be used to prepare *saus kacang*, or peanut sauce, for *satay*.

Fryer or boiler Both terms refer to chickens which are 10–16 weeks old and weigh 450 g–1.35 kg (1–3 lb).

Chilli In the United States, as a result of Mexican influence, the word "chilli" is often synonymous with chilli powder, which is stocked in every supermarket and grocery. Chilli powder is a mildly sharp and piquant mixture comprising paprika, cumin, oregano, salt, garlic and Cayenne pepper. The use of chilli powder in Indonesian cooking would result in a disaster. In this book, "chillies" refer to what North Americans generally know as "hot peppers".

Soy sauce In Indonesian cooking, sweet soy sauce is *kecap manis*, but dark soy sauce is *kecap asin* or salty soy sauce. There is a great difference between them and in Indonesian cooking, sweet soy sauce is an absolute must. If, for example, you use Chinese dark soy sauce, which is very salty, and if it is used with salt added to the recipe, we will have a monumental culinary disaster.

Ingredients For all the recipes in this book, use **ground** cloves, cumin, turmeric, coriander, galangal (*laos*), black pepper and grated nutmeg unless specified otherwise.

Sambal oelek Many of the recipes call for *sambal oelek*. The recipe for *sambal oelek* can be found on page 159.

Terasi Also known as *belacan*, *terasi* is a very pungent ingredient made from dried prawns (shrimps). Use very sparingly, even the smallest, pea-sized amount will add a distinct flavour to the dish.

17

Where to Buy

Many of the so-called 'exotic' ingredients used in the preparation of Indonesian dishes, such as dried prawn (shrimp) paste or *terasi* and lemon grass, are readily obtainable outside of Southeast Asia. With today's Internet facilities, finding sources for ingredients is easier and quicker than ever before. Also, in American supermarkets, items that were once exotic are now commonplace. When I first came to Connecticut, a banana was the most exotic thing I could find. It's hard to imagine that I can now find different varieties of bananas, lemon grass, lychees (litchis) and even durian at the local Stop & Shop.

Immeasurable Delight

This book is intended as a simplified guide through the labyrinth of a form of Asian cooking unknown generally in the West and in large parts of Asia, yet possessing a stature comparable to the renown of Chinese and French styles of cooking.

The reader should not accept each recipe in this volume as dogma. Cooking is an art, not a science. Ten cooks working with the same recipe will produce ten variations on a theme, some better and some worse. All a cookbook can really do is mark the guidelines and provide the reader with instructions for the preparation of specific dishes. The execution of the dish, however, is entirely in the hands of the cook. It is all a matter of personal taste. If a recipe calls for one teaspoon of ginger, the object of the author has been merely to convey to you that it is generally the amount used. Some persons may prefer slightly more ginger; others, slightly less. Similarly, the meat you purchase on one occasion may not be as tender as on the next. Every cook knows this and also knows that this can affect the outcome of a dish.

While these observations may appear commonplace, I should like to stress again that the recipes in this book should not be taken literally. I have observed Indonesian cooks at work from the village to the palace level. They do not use graduated cups, scales and the paraphernalia commonplace in the machinery-cluttered modern kitchen. Intuitively, but actually as a result of trial and error, accompanied by an artistic flair, Indonesian cooks have put together some truly remarkable dishes by rule of thumb.

At all times, a recipe must be tasted to a happy conclusion. This is especially true when you are working with a variety of spices. A little more of this and less of that — do not be afraid to use your fingers. Keep tasting as you go along.

Introduction: Points of Origin

For the gourmet, Indonesia, the Spice Islands of antiquity, may be likened to a kaleidoscope of Asian cookery. Indonesian food is an exciting blend of Muslim, Hindu and Buddhist influences. Expressed differently, it is a melding of Malay-Arab, Indian and Chinese culinary arts. In brilliant fashion, the Indonesians have subtly combined these contrasting influences and, primarily through the judicious use of the very spices which gave the islands their name, have developed a unique form of cookery.

The Indonesian centrepiece is the *rijsttafel*, in literal translation "rice table", a Dutch-minted phrase which has come into common usage throughout the islands. Once a rare epicurean experience, the *rijsttafel* can today be easily duplicated in the modern, Western-type kitchen. Essentially, a rice table consists of a mound of rice in an individual bowl, garnished with samplings of fifty or more peripheral dishes. The *rijsttafel* is ideal for a buffet, a sort of tropical, Asian smorgasbord.

The dishes composing the rice table range from familiar fishes in unfamiliar sauces to curried fowls, skewered cubes of lamb and pork, and vegetables skillfully blended with spices. The *rijsttafel* moved the late Miguel Covarrubias, the outstanding Mexican illustrator and author, to observe that "the food that Balinese gourmets eat at festivals is as elaborate as any in the world". Indeed, it is. As a brochure of the former Hotel des Indes, once known as the gateway to the Indies, noted, "to be fully appreciated, the *rijsttafel* must be experienced — and the greater the experience, the greater the appreciation".

To appreciate the *rijsttafel*, one must appreciate its place of origin. To begin with, the islands of Indonesia are fashioned like a jade necklace, extending from the tip of Southeast Asia to the northern coastline of Australia. The archipelago is the world's largest and it contains literally thousands of islands, or beads, to complete the metaphor. The names have a familiar ring: Sumatra, Java, Kalimantan (Borneo), Sulawesi (Celebes), Maluku (the Moluccas) and the fabled Bali.

Westerners as well as Chinese and Indian travellers have been tempted by the epicurean delights of the islanders for centuries. In the thirteenth century, for example, the intrepid Marco Polo, after a twenty-year sojourn in Cathay, sailed for Europe by way of the island chain. His frail ship sailed among the islands for several months. An inveterate noter, he amassed a collection of recipes and spices. Indeed, he gave the archipelago the sobriquet "Spice Islands". In this region of the globe, he wrote, is "obtained the greatest part of the spices that are distributed throughout the world". Among them he listed pepper, nutmeg and clove. He apparently enjoyed Indonesian cooking. On Sumatra, for example, he found that people ate flesh "clean and unclean"; among the clean, as today, buffalo and wild swine; among the unclean, the crocodile. In my part of the tropical world, the Amazon, we still eat lizard, the iguana; doubtless, Marco Polo would consider it "unclean".

The Genoese traveller was an accurate and descriptive writer. For example, imagine the Western reaction to his report of an Indonesian nut, which contains "an edible substance that is sweet and pleasant to the taste, and white as milk". The cavity of the pulp, he said, was filled with liquid — clear as water, cool and better flavoured and more delicate than wine, or any other kind of drink whatever. The nut? The coconut, of course.

As for eating habits on the islands, he observed that the people produced "no wheat, but lived on rice". He also discovered that there were no grapes and, therefore, no wines in the archipelago but sensibilities were assured when he learned of a species of tree resembling the date-bearing palm from which the Indonesians procured "an excellent beverage". He then proceeded to give the recipe for palm wine.

Things have not changed that much since then in the Indonesian kitchen. Today, as yesterday, the people still "live on rice". In the words of an Indonesian government authority, "A meal is not a meal unless there is rice." But rice is only the plinth upon which the *rijsttafel* is constructed. All told, there are 1,000 Indonesian recipes, more or less; invariably, rice is at the base of all of them.

This brings us back to the question of just precisely what is a *rijsttafel*? Among foreigners in Indonesia, the big rice table has become a Sunday ritual. Properly served in the old days, the drama develops like this. A headwaiter approaches the table carrying a huge bowl of steaming white rice, followed by an Indian file of as many as thirty waiters, each bearing a deep bowl or oval platter, or sometimes a lazy susan. Each plate or compartment contains a different dish.

First you build a small mound of rice in the centre of your bowl. Then, as each waiter files by, you take a helping from his tray. The mound of food, which starts like a knoll, gradually grows into a veritable mountain. As the last waiter moves to the adjoining table to repeat the process (much to your relief), the dining commences.

There is no formal procedure in putting together a rice bowl. Some people try to keep each sample of food separate (a hopeless task); others mix everything together with an air of carefree abandon and top the dish with peanut sauce. In any event, each spoonful — the *rijsttafel* is eaten primarily with a spoon and fork, but no knife — provides a unique taste sensation. Although most Indonesians are nominally Muslim and prefer either water or a soft drink with their meal, a tall, frosty glass of beer is highly recommended. Indeed, it is mandatory.

In these hurried days, the *rijsttafel* has devolved into a buffet. Most of Indonesia's new, modern hotels serve it in this manner. I suppose self-service is egalitarian, in tune with the age. It certainly is less elegant, although I must concede that at village feasts, especially on the outer islands, the buffet style reigns supreme.

The unique character of the *rijsttafel* is not born solely of variety. If it were merely a question of preparing different kinds of dishes, a rice table would simply be a super French *hors d'oeuvres* or Italian *antipasto*. But the portions in a *rijsttafel* are far more generous and a couple of dishes with rice could easily constitute a full meal.

Perhaps in no other form of cooking is there such a prolific use of spices, in a variety of combinations with results ranging from fiery to sweet and mild. In some ways, Indonesian cooking is like opening a spice safe. If you know the proper combination, the door swings open easily.

One piece of Western nonsense must be dispensed with immediately. Among the uninitiated, the mistaken notion arises that spices necessarily denote "hot" food. That may be the case but it is not necessarily true. Some spices are decidedly sweet, others are simply aromatic; some are mild and, of course, others unforgettably searing.

Spices, of course, have been employed in the kitchen since the first campfire. The Aztecs and the Egyptians used them with sophistication. Both the Bible and the Koran have references to them. Nowhere, however, is there a more natural spice chamber than on the islands of Indonesia, where people have cultivated spice gardens since time immemorial. Centuries of usage have refined the employment of spices in their culinary art to the point of perfection.

Let us briefly examine some of the more familiar spices, which we shall be using in the pages ahead. Perhaps the best known, and most popular spice, is the pepper vine, a perennial climbing shrub that is widely cultivated in southern Sumatra, in Kalimantan (Borneo) and on the islands of Bangka and Billiton, situated in the Java-Singapore-Sumatra triangle. Most cooks distinguish between black and white pepper. Black pepper is simply unripened, dried pepper. White pepper is the familiar black pepper, but unhulled. There is still another pepper: the red variety, also green sometimes. Oddly enough, red pepper is unrelated to the pepper vine. It is generally known as chilli and the dried form as Cayenne pepper, after the capital of French Guiana which adjoins my native Surinam.

It is an incendiary spice. In fact, our South American variety is hotter than the Southeast Asian and I have confirmed this by trying it out on Achenese friends. They boast about their ability to consume flaming hot food.

Invariably, the hotter the climate, the hotter is the food. This is a generally accepted axiom. Hot food is supposed to ventilate the body, acting as a sort of air-conditioner. There are exceptions to the axiom, however. Inexplicably, Korean food is hot.

About a decade ago, the National Geographic Society in the United States sent two travellers, Helen and Frank Schreider, to Indonesia. Their first Indonesian meal with an Indonesian family was memorable. They wrote:

"We want you to try Indonesian food," our host said, heaping our plates with steaming *satay*, a miniature kebab; flaky chips of *krupuk*, ground shrimp; *gado-gado*, a vegetable dish with peanut sauce; and mounds of boiled, white rice.

"The food is not spicy enough," she advised us. "You must add your own *sambal*, our Indonesian pepper sauce."

Both Helen and I like hot food and I used the *sambal* liberally. The result was as explosive as the eruption of Krakatoa, Indonesia's famous volcano. Blinded by tears, I groped for the tea in a frantic effort to put out the fire.

This, alas, is the usual introduction to spices. But then there are the sweet and aromatic spices such as cinnamon, a member of the laurel family. Some of the Indonesian trees, which still yield an abundance of the bark from which cinnamon is processed, are older than the American and French Revolutions. My husband contends, however, that the cinnamon of Vietnam rivals that of Java. Another sweet or mild spice closely related to cinnamon is cassia. And still another is the nutmeg, the evergreen which grows wild in Maluku (the Moluccas) and whose outer covering is used in the kitchen under the name of mace. It may seem out of place to write of evergreens in the tropics but they are there.

Another spice-producing evergreen is the clove tree. It sometimes grows more than 9.1 metres (30 feet) in height; at least it does on Ambon. It has clusters of yellow-pink flowers, which are picked when the colour turns brick-red. Indonesians are particularly fond of the nail-shaped cloves.

Incidentally, the aroma of cloves hangs heavy over most of Indonesia, like a smog, but a far more pleasant smog than that of London or Los Angeles. I am not exaggerating about this smog business and the cause is relatively understandable. Indonesians delight in mixing cloves in their cigarette tobacco. Every time an Indonesian lights up (and there are almost one hundred million chain-smokers on the islands), the cigarette smoke gives off an aroma of cloves. Imagine hundreds of millions tiny rolls of paper, cloves and tobacco going up in smoke daily! The spice smog is especially noticeable in the *desa* or village areas, away from the cities and their ubiquitous combustible engines.

Another spice frequently used in Indonesian cooking which is far from hot is ginger. We used to grow ginger in our garden in Java not simply for the ginger, which is taken from the bulbous root, but for the lovely purplish flowers they produce. Closely related to ginger is turmeric, which is native to Indonesia and indispensable in Indian and Pakistani cooking. Its colour and taste vary from place to place throughout southern Asia. Only the turmeric of Bengal can match that of Indonesia. Turmeric, of course, is basic in the preparation of curry. Indeed, many of the other spices which go into curries are found on the Spice Islands, including cardamom (usually misspelt as "cardamon") and cumin, which has a slightly bitter (not hot) taste and is used in the West for pickling and sausage making.

The brief review of spices would be incomplete without another favourite found in the Indonesian kitchen: coriander. The 'seeds' are crushed, thereby producing one of the most fragrant of all spices. Coriander leaves (cilantro) are often used for curries. The famous Chinese parsley is simply coriander leaves. According to legend, coriander has the power of a love potion. I suspect it is widely used on the islands as an aphrodisiac.

Lastly, the Indonesian spice shelf includes various leaves such as the *salam* leaf, which has the taste of bitter almonds, and *serai* or lemon grass. In Indonesia, *serai* is used either dry or fresh.

I have run through the gamut of the more popular Indonesian spices because of the dramatic roles they play in the preparation of a *rijsttafel*. Obviously, the preparation of a rice table can be a major undertaking. However, the recipes in this book have been especially selected so that small *rijsttafels* or buffets may be easily prepared as zestful substitutes for otherwise common dishes. The ingredients mentioned in the recipes to follow are, of course, readily obtainable in Southeast Asia. In Australia, Japan or the West, the suggestion is simply to write to the local Indonesian embassy and inquire as to their sources of raw materials. Indonesian missions abroad invariably serve Indonesian food and they usually have the address of a local distributor. However, you will find that it is not difficult to obtain Indonesian ingredients in Britain, America or elsewhere.

As you will notice later on, unlike most Chinese, Western and Indian cookbooks, the recipes that follow do not specifically suggest how many people may be served from one dish. The reason is that Indonesian dinners consist of many dishes. As a general rule, four persons may eat well if the *rijsttafel* consists of rice, one chicken, one *satay* dish and one vegetable dish. For each additional couple, add one dish. Of course, after a while, you may wish to make larger portions of some dishes and smaller ones of others. Each recipe in this book is designed to complete a simple, easily prepared rice table of rice plus three other dishes. With rice, when you have Asians at dinner, the amount consumed is double or triple that when only Westerners are seated at the table. Asians offset this, however, by not eating much meat or fish. The Occidentals go skimpy on the rice and fill their bowls generously with everything else in sight.

I keep referring to the rice table as Indonesian, which it is but nobody really knows of its origin, that is, how it came about. Marco Polo, for example, does not touch on the subject. Some historians have speculated (as historians are wont to do) that the *rijsttafel* as the Indonesians know it today did not exist in their time. Significantly, for that matter, Sir Stamford Raffles, the founder of Singapore, administrator, botanist and historian extraordinary, did not mention it in his two-volume history of Java. The probability, however, is that his notes about and recipes from the Indonesian kitchen were lost at sea, together with his collection of flora and fauna, when one of his ships foundered in a monsoon off the west coast of Sumatra. Speculation is irresistible.

The late Emily Hahn, a popular authoress of her time, argued that the rice table is a relatively recent development dating from about the start of the nineteenth century. She contended that the colonising Dutch avoided rice when they first settled in the East Indies. With characteristic conservativeness, the Hollanders are supposed to have approached Indonesian food with a degree of temerity, first tasting one dish, then sampling another. The Dutch were indecisive and simply added one dish to another over the centuries until the full *rijsttafel* emerged. This story has a touch of the Charles Lamb ring to it. Miss Hahn, however, provided some evidence that the *rijsttafel* was full blown by the time of the Napoleonic Wars, when Raffles was the Lieutenant-Governor of Java. She quoted from a letter written by Victor Ido van de Wall in 1812 and it described a Dutch breakfast in those days as consisting of "warm rice, curry, fish, beefsteak, *dendeng* (dried meat), Macassar fish, peppers, greens (and) roast chicken, lavishly washed down with red wine, beer, Madeira, Rhine wine, brandy and seltzer water". A Lucullian meal, indeed. The Dutch are justly famous for their appetites but what could conceivably have constituted lunch or dinner after a breakfast of those dimensions? Whatever the case, the de Wall description has the earmarks of today's rice table.

No matter what the origins of Indonesian cookery — from Hindu invaders, Arab traders, Chinese settlers or Dutch colonisers — the art of Indonesian cooking holds the prospect of new horizons for the gourmet. It is a gustatory challenge worth accepting.

Rice:
The Main Prop

Rice requires little introduction. *Oryza sativa linn* is more than the Asian stuff of life: it is a gift of the gods. At least it is on Java, where it is revered as the offspring of Dewi Sri, a goddess. No festival in Indonesia is complete without rice in some form. On some islands, rice dolls are fashioned from the stalk of the plant and given as good-luck pieces to brides and pregnant women; I once sent my sister-in-law a rice doll from Bali and apparently it worked. This relationship between rice and fecundity, by the way, is not merely a quaint bit of Asian folklore. In the West, no church wedding is complete without a handful of rice thrown at the retreating bride and groom.

The place of origin of rice is open to considerable speculation, although the trend among botanists is to cite Southeast Asia as the native habitat. Here, at least, there is no doubt that rice grows in a wild state. From Southeast Asia, it is presumed to have travelled westward into India, Persia, Egypt, Greece and Rome, and northward into China, Korea and Japan. In the West, rice is relatively a late development; the Bible does not mention it. We do know, however, that in 1685, it was introduced into South Carolina. Today, the United States is a leading rice producer and exporter but still not a consumer.

Rice varies in size and taste from region to region. It is a matter of personal preference but I prefer the Indonesian, Burmese, Vietnamese and South Chinese varieties. In Indonesia, a superb rice is grown on the Krawang delta situated between Jakarta and Ciribon, along the northern coastline of Java. Among the better kinds of rice must be listed the long-grain, white variety grown in the American South, usually in Arkansas, Louisiana or the Carolinas.

Unfortunately, many people are easily terrified at the thought of cooking rice. Too often, professionals (restaurant cooks), semi-professionals (home cooks) and amateur chefs concoct something termed "rice" but more easily identified as bookbinder's paste. How often, even in a euphemistically characterised 'Chinese' restaurant, have you been served soggy, sticky glutinous rice with each grain clinging desperately to the other so that the end product is an unrecognisable, unappetising white mass of mush? Properly prepared, each grain of rice should stand by itself, separate and distinct, like tiny grains of sand on a beach. Rice cookery would seem to compare with the interminable conflict between man and the mob.

The truth, however, is that rice is relatively simple to cook. There are a few basic rules that any child can follow. Kitty (Cathay), our daughter, can cook rice without difficulty and she has been doing so since she was nine. Since rice is the plinth of the Asian meal — whether Indonesian, Chinese or Sri Lankan — no Oriental epicurean edifice can be erected without it. Thus, the mastery of rice cookery is mandatory.

My suggestion to the beginner is to disregard completely the invariably misleading instructions found on packaged rice. It is inexplicable why these firms persist in prescribing mucilage recipes for rice recipes. Perhaps more perplexing is why home cooks persist in pursuing instructions which they know by experience simply will not work. The beginner should also bear in mind several basic pointers. Never use too large a pot for cooking rice and never fill the pot more than one-third full with uncooked rice. If you must use an aluminium pot, carefully observe the special instructions for it.

The basic cause of most trouble in rice cookery is the pot. In China, India and Pakistan, copper and brass pots are preferred; in Indonesia and most of Southeast Asia, the iron pot. In some places, a trivet is used for good measure, for example in South America. These reasons will be explained shortly. The important point in this brief introduction to rice is that it is a great dish when properly made and that it can be easily prepared.

Next time you open a packet of rice, remember that 3 billion people eat rice every day at every meal — and apparently they do not encounter too much trouble in its preparation. No, they do not tire of it, no more than a Westerner tires of eating wheat in one form or another every day at almost every meal during his life.

COOKING RICE The selection of the type and size of the pot or saucepan is the critical factor in the preparation of rice. The pot should be of thick metal: iron, copper or an alloy of brass and copper. The decisive element is the bottom, which is the surface exposed to the fire. If the bottom is made from thick or heavy metal, it shields the rice from burning and singeing — a common failure.

In the West, the most common culinary metal is aluminium. This could mean disaster in cooking rice. The walls of an aluminium pot are too thin and the heat penetrates intensely. But this problem is easily surmounted. The secret is to place an old-fashioned potato baker or cookie sheet over the range burner and then place the aluminium pot on top of it. The addition of this slim piece of extra metal between the flame and the bottom of the aluminium pot shields the bottom of the pot and reduces the heat tremendously. At home, in the interior of jungle-cloaked Surinam, which abuts on the Amazon and where aluminium pots are the fashion (Surinam has the world's largest reserve of bauxite, the red-rich loam from which aluminium is processed), my mother places a cast-iron trivet between the flame and the aluminium pot.

Using the potato baker, cookie sheet or trivet necessitates an additional 15 minutes of cooking, but the results are infallible. Such a cooking device, known as the "flame tamer" or "flame master", is available in any American department store.

In addition to the problem of selecting the correct utensil, another important factor in the preparation of rice — often overlooked — is the size of the pot. Too large a pot should be avoided. The uncooked rice should fill only one-third the volume of the pot. The cooked rice will fill the vacant area as it expands during the cooking process.

Having selected the correct pot, put 400 g (2 cups) of rice in the pot and wash twice under cold tap water. Now, drain and add 625 ml (2½ cups) of cold water. Stir well with a fork and cover tightly. Place the pot over low heat and cook for about 45 minutes. Then, stir once with a fork, replace cover and cook another 15 minutes. The moisture should now be completely absorbed by the grains.

A last tip: it is always better to have less water than too much. If the rice is not cooked enough at the end of the specified cooking time, you can always sprinkle or gently add in more water and cook the rice a little longer. Too much water, however, results in a soggy mass of mucilaginous quality.

One pound or 450 g of rice, properly cooked, should make four to six servings, accompanied by Indonesian side-dishes. See the recipe for Nasi Putih (Plain White Rice) for an alternative method. Either method may be used with confidence.

Of course, having an electric rice-cooker will make your life easier, but it is good to know how to really cook a dish from scratch. Even today, if making rice for myself or just two or three people, I will eschew the electric and go back to my old way. The end result is not necessarily the same. Maybe it's just me but when I cook the rice the 'old-fashioned' way, I think the taste is less soggy and the grains are tastier.

Nasi Putih ✦
(Plain White Rice)

Ingredients

Long-grain rice	400 g (2 cups)
Water	625 ml (2½ cups)

Method

- Wash rice twice under cold tap water. Drain.
- Transfer rice to a saucepan and add water. Bring to the boil and simmer uncovered until all liquid has been absorbed.
- Cover saucepan, lower heat and cook for 15 minutes more.

Nasi Kuning ✦
(Yellow Rice)

Ingredients

Long-grain rice	400 g (2 cups)
Coconut milk	625 ml (2½ cups), squeezed from 1 grated coconut with sufficient water added
Turmeric (*kunyit*)	1 tsp, ground
Coriander (*ketumbar*)	½ tsp, ground
Salam leaf (*daun salam*)	1
Garlic	2 cloves, peeled and chopped
Salt	2 tsp
Onion	1, large, peeled and sliced
Vegetable oil	1 Tbsp
Cucumber	1, medium, peeled and cut into long strips

Method

- Wash rice twice and drain. Transfer to a saucepan and add coconut milk, turmeric, coriander, *salam* leaf, garlic and salt. Cook, covered tightly, over medium heat.
- Meanwhile, fry onion slices in oil.
- Garnish cooked rice with fried onion slices and cucumber strips. Serve.

Nasi Guri ✦
(Fragrant Rice)

Nasi Guri is prepared in Indonesia on special occasions like festivals, Islamic holidays, birthdays and weddings.

Ingredients

Long-grain rice	400 g (2 cups)
Coconut milk	625 ml (2½ cups), squeezed from 1 grated coconut with sufficient water added
Salam leaves (*daun salam*)	2
Salt	2 tsp

Garnishing

Onion	1, large, peeled, sliced and fried in oil until brown and crispy
Vegetable oil or margarine	3 Tbsp
Eggs	2
Milk	1 Tbsp
Salt	a pinch
Cucumber	1, small, peeled and thinly sliced
Spicy coconut balls	1 recipe, see pg 142

Method

- Wash rice twice and drain.
- Transfer rice to a saucepan and add coconut milk, *salam* leaves and salt. Bring to the boil and simmer uncovered until all liquid has been absorbed.
- Cover saucepan, lower heat and cook for 15 minutes more.
- While rice is cooking, prepare garnishing. Fry onion slices in oil or margarine until brown and crisp. Set aside.
- Make an omelette from eggs, adding milk and salt. Cut omelette into strips and set aside.
- Lastly, prepare cucumber and make spicy coconut balls.
- After rice is cooked, transfer to an oval platter and garnish. Serve.

Nasi Ayam ✎
(Chicken and Rice)

Ingredients

Chicken	1, about 1.15 kg (2 lb 8 oz), quartered
Salt	2½ Tbsp
Salam leaf (*daun salam*)	1
Cinnamon (*kayu manis*)	1 stick, 5 cm (2 inches) in length
Coconut milk	750 ml (3 cups), squeezed from 1 grated coconut with sufficient water added
Long-grain rice	400 g (2 cups)

Method

- Wash and clean chicken thoroughly, then put into a heavy saucepan. Add salt, *salam* leaf, cinnamon stick and 500 ml (2 cups) coconut milk. Cover tightly and cook over medium heat for about 30 minutes.
- Remove chicken from stock. Add remaining coconut milk, stir and measure out 625 ml (2½ cups) of liquid to reserve.
- Wash rice twice and drain completely. Put rice into a saucepan, then add reserved liquid and cook rice.
- Add chicken after rice has cooked for 30 minutes, then steam for an additional 15 minutes or until done.
- When serving, bury chicken in the rice.

Nasi Ulam ✎
(Rice and Spice)

Ingredients

Long-grain rice	400 g (2 cups)
Onion	1, small, peeled and chopped
Garlic	2 cloves, peeled and chopped
Vegetable oil	2 Tbsp
Cumin (*jintan*)	a pinch, ground
Coriander (*ketumbar*)	1 tsp, ground
Red chilli	½, crushed
Lemon grass (*serai*)	½ tsp, ground
Salt	2 tsp
Kaffir lime leaves (*daun jeruk purut*)	2
Dried prawn (shrimp) paste (*terasi*)	1 pea-size piece
Coconut milk	625 ml (2½ cups), squeezed from 1 grated coconut with sufficient water added

Method

- Wash rice twice, drain and set aside.
- Sauté chopped onion and garlic in oil. Add cumin, coriander, crushed red chilli, lemon grass and salt. Stir well.
- Add in rice and stir continuously until thoroughly mixed with spicy ingredients. Add lime leaves and dried prawn paste.
- Add coconut milk and bring to the boil, allowing to simmer until all liquid is absorbed. Then, cover, reduce heat and cook for 15 minutes more.
- This dish may be garnished with fried onion, peeled and sliced cucumber, an egg omelette cut into strips, or a handful of fried peanuts.

Nasi Kebuli ∂

(Fragrant Rice and Chicken)

Ingredients

Chicken	1, about 1.15 kg (2 lb 8 oz), quartered
Lemon grass (*serai*)	1 tsp, ground
Galangal (*laos*)	½ tsp, ground
Coriander (*ketumbar*)	½ tsp, ground
Kaffir lime leaves (*daun jeruk purut*)	3
Garlic	2 cloves, peeled and chopped
Salt	1 Tbsp
Water	500 ml (2 cups)
Vegetable oil	3 Tbsp
Long-grain rice	400 g (2 cups), washed twice and drained
Nutmeg (*pala*)	a pinch, grated
Ginger	a pinch, ground
Black peppercorns	4
Mace (*sekar pala*)	2 pieces
Onions	2, medium, peeled, sliced and fried in oil until medium brown

Method

- Wash and clean chicken. Put into a heavy saucepan, then add lemon grass, galangal, coriander, kaffir lime leaves, garlic, salt and water. Cover tightly and cook until chicken is tender.
- Remove chicken from stock, reserving it for later use. Fry chicken in oil until golden brown and set aside.
- Put rice into a saucepan, add 625 ml (2½ cups) chicken stock, nutmeg, ginger, peppercorns and mace and cook rice until all liquid has been absorbed.
- Cover, lower heat and cook for 15 minutes more. Transfer cooked rice to a large platter and arrange aromatic chicken on the sides. Alternatively, divide into individual portions.
- Garnish with fried onion slices. Serve.

Opposite: Nasi Kebuli

Lontong ∂

(Rice in Banana Leaves)

Ingredients

Long-grain rice	400 g (2 cups)
Banana leaves	
Bamboo toothpicks or cocktail sticks	
Water	2.5 litres (10 cups / 4 pints)

Method

- Wash rice twice and drain. Portion and place onto banana leaves, then fold into secure oblong packets and fasten with toothpicks.
- Boil banana leaf-packets in 2.5 litres water for about 3 hours. It may be necessary to add more water during this period.

OR

Ingredients

Long-grain rice	200 g (1 cup)
Water	500 ml (2 cups)
Banana leaves	
Bamboo toothpicks or cocktail sticks	

Method

- Wash rice twice, drain and transfer to a saucepan. Add water and boil rice until soft.
- Place onto banana leaves, roll into oblongs and fasten with toothpicks. Place into a pot and fill with 500 ml water. Boil for 1 hour.
- Leave to cool, slice and serve. *Lontong* is a good accompaniment for dishes like Gado-gado or a *sambal*.

NOTE: In the West or wherever banana leaves are hard to come by, use aluminium foil or corn husks as wrappers.

Nasi Goreng
(Fried Rice, Indonesian Style)

Ingredients

Long-grain rice	400 g (2 cups)
Water	625 ml (2½ cups)
Salt	2 tsp
Chicken breast	1, diced
Vegetable oil or margarine	2 Tbsp
Onions	2, large, peeled and sliced
Garlic	2 cloves, peeled and chopped
Coriander (*ketumbar*)	½ tsp, ground
Galangal (*laos*)	½ tsp, ground
Dried prawn (shrimp) paste (*terasi*)	1 pea-size piece
Red chilli	1, crushed
Sweet soy sauce (*kecap manis*)	2 Tbsp
Cooked prawns (shrimps)	about 225 g (1 cup)
Fried egg (optional)	1

Method

- Wash rice twice and drain. Transfer to a saucepan and add water and salt. Bring to the boil and simmer uncovered until all liquid has been absorbed.

- Cover, lower heat and cook for 15 minutes more. After rice is cooked, set aside until sufficiently cool.

- Fry diced chicken in oil or margarine until light brown. Add sliced onions and sauté with chicken until onions brown.

- Lower heat and add chopped garlic, coriander, galangal and dried prawn paste. Stir well and add crushed red chilli. Fry about 1 minute.

- Add soy sauce and prawns, mixing thoroughly. Finally, add pre-cooked rice. Maintain a low, steady heat and stir constantly until rice turns light brown.

- In Indonesia, Nasi Goreng Istimewa (Fried Rice Special) is fried rice topped with a fried egg.

NOTE: Though chicken and prawns are used in this recipe, any kind of meat or fish will do as well, as long as it is properly diced.

Fish and Other Seafood

Indonesia is the largest archipelago in the world, embracing 1,903,650 square kilometres of islands and seas. Its water abound in seafood: fishes, prawns, mollusks, turtles and other forms of sea life. As elsewhere in Southeast Asia, fish and prawns are served either grilled, roasted or sautéed in spicy sauces. They are also ground fine, dried on mats in the sun, mixed with sea-water, permitted to ferment and then made into an acrid, pungent, rich paste. In Indonesia, this paste is called *terasi* and is found in almost every Indonesian dish. It can be either inexpensively purchased from importers in the Western world or substituted with anchovy paste. In Indonesia, the odour of *terasi* permeates the kitchen.

"I was to find this a daily smell, punctual and inevitable as the morning smell of coffee at home," the late Colin McPhee, the musicologist and former Balinese resident, wrote. "It was unbelievably putrid. An amount the size of a pea was more than enough to flavour a dish. It gave a racy, briny tang to the food and I soon found myself craving it as an animal craves salt."

Some of the fishes of Indonesia are exotic but many of them are familiar on the Chinese or Western dinner table — sardines, summer flounder (fluke), halibut, bonito, mackerel, school tuna and anchovies. They may be found in many of the Indonesian ports, which stud the coastline. Each seaside village boasts a *pasar ikan* or fish market of its own. As soon as the graceful, sea-going prau with enormous eyes painted on their port and starboard bow (so that the vessel can 'see' where she is sailing) arrives in a harbour, the fish are unloaded and briskly sold. Often, street-hawkers will buy up the catch, string the fish through the gills along a bamboo pole and then trudge down the nearest dusty roads for the inland villages, shouting their wares on the way. People on Chinese bicycles will also suddenly appear on the scene to buy up basketfuls of fish, rushing them to the big towns.

Perhaps the pièce de résistance among Indonesian saltwater catches is the *kakap*, a giant sea perch and member of the marine bass family, which tastes like fillet of sole — only better. In hotels and restaurants, *kakap à la meuniere* is a favourite on the menu. The *kakap* inhabits the muddy coastline and is sometimes taken in big freshwater rivers such as the Solo which courses through central Java. Another Indonesian favourite is the *gurami*, or gourami, a type of carp. It is to the island's freshwater fishes what *kakap* is to the saltwater varieties. Every village has its gourami pond; curried or sautéed in spices, gourami is an especially fine dish. No rice table is complete without one fish course and *kakap* or gourami usually fills the bill; in the West, porgy and sea bass are ideal substitutes.

At Bagangsiapiapi, on the east coast of Sumatra, Indonesia once boasted the largest fishing port in the world and the waters of eastern Indonesia are still a fisherman's paradise. East of the imaginary Wallace line, which flows through the Macassar Strait and which divides the flora and fauna of Indonesia between Asia and Oceania, the islands lose their Asian characteristics and assume the appearance of the South Sea islands of the Joseph Conrad and Robert Louis Stevenson epics. The Macassar Strait and the waters

around Sulawesi, Banda and Maluku are favourite haunts of the fork-tail fishes: bonito, tuna and mackerel.

Bonito, called *tongkol* or *jakalong*, abound in eastern Indonesia. They appear in schools and are often caught on chicken feather lures. On the picturesque island of Ambon, bonito is served at breakfast with rice and spices — a distant cry from bacon and eggs. Tuna is also plentiful. The Indonesians call them *abu-abu* (ash-ash) or *tonny*, a derivative of the Dutch word *tonjin*. Mackerel is another familiar fish and can be found anywhere from the Sangir Talaud islands south of the Philippines to the coast of east Java. Cooked in coconut or peanut oil, the mackerel or *banjar* (as the Javanese call it) is an epicurean treat.

Although the flat-fishes such as the fluke and flounder enjoy immense popularity in the West, the Indonesians tend to treat them with disdain, perhaps because of their unusual appearance. The largest and most frequently caught flatfish in the archipelago is the *langkau*, a relative of halibut of the Grand Banks off Canada's eastern coast. Another familiar fish, introduced with considerable success by the Chinese, is the carp. The Chinese must have brought with them some prize specimens from Cathay. The finest I have ever seen was in a pond at the home of an Indonesian of Chinese ancestry in Celebes, or Sulawesi as the Indonesians now call the octopus-shaped island. In Indonesia, the carp is appropriately called *ikan emas* or gold fish, although carp lose their gold colouring as they mature. In west Java, in the hilly country beyond Bogor, there are innumerable *ikan emas* ponds and peddlers of *ikan emas* take their wares from town to town.

The waters of Indonesia have other familiar fishes, such as the *ikan kakaktua* (named after the parrot-like *kakaktua* bird), which is similar to black-fish. It has a strong beak and a mouth rimmed with a full set of teeth. Then there is the sailfish, which the Indonesians call similarly: *ikan* (fish) *lajar* (sail). Another is the *bandeng* which is a cross between the salmon and a distant cousin of the herring; smoked, *bandeng* is one of the great dishes of the world. Other popular Indonesian fishes, invariably cooked in spices, are the *kuro*, which reminds me of a barracuda, and the *lajang*, which has the appearance of a Caribbean jack-fish.

A survey of Indonesia's table fishes would be incomplete without a passing mention of the small fishes, such as *ikan teri* or anchovy, and the *lemuru* or sardine, which are so popular on the islands. Dried and salted, they are used to garnish various dishes. On the Western-type cocktail circuit, dried *ikan teri* in particular makes a tasty titbit, especially with a gimlet. (Note: A proper gimlet is four parts gin and one part lemon squash, not lemon juice. In recent years, alas, the British-invented gimlet has lost its popularity in Southeast Asia and as I discovered on my last trip, in Kuala Lumpur, Singapore, and the northern Bornean states, the martini has become increasingly fashionable. I found this rather disappointing since a martini invariably tastes better before a crackling log fire with deep snow on the ground outside and icy winds buffeting the house. Be that as it may.)

Of course, there are other forms of seafood used in the Indonesian kitchen. Prawns or shrimps are in great abundance. They are not only made into paste, but are often fried in coconut oil with spices. Prawns are also skewered, *satay*-style. In the old Kota section of Jakarta, near the Dutch drawbridges and forts built 300 years ago, a wide variety of shellfish and giant sea turtles are available. This is the area known as *Pasar Ikan*, a kind of Fulton Fish Market, which is a must for anyone interested in Indonesian cookery.

Squids and tiny octopuses are also available and they are kitchen favourites on the islands. In the following section, however, I have omitted the quaint delicacies such as octopus. By experience, I have found that Westerners tend to avoid them and, in any event, they are not generally available in most Western fish markets, Italian and Spanish markets excepted. Moreover, Europeans and Americans invariably eat almost the same kinds of fish as the Indonesians, give or take a fin here or there. Accordingly, I have kept to the popular fishes, such as porgy (scup), sea bass, mackerel, bonito, carp, cod and smelt. For a really big fish, the striped bass, cooked in soy sauce, is a masterpiece. At a Christmas party some years ago, we featured a striped bass, which my husband, an incurable fisherman, caught off Montauk Point, Long Island, opposite our Connecticut shoreline. It proved very successful.

Ikan Kecap ❧

(Soy Fish)

Ingredients

Whole fish	1, about 450–700 g (1 lb–1 lb 8 oz) dressed weight, preferably porgy, sea bass or gourami
Salt	1 tsp
Vegetable oil	2 Tbsp
Garlic	2 cloves, peeled and coarsely chopped
Onion	1, large, peeled and coarsely chopped
Sambal oelek (see pg 159)	1 tsp
Sweet soy sauce (*kecap manis*)	2 Tbsp
Ginger	a pinch, ground
Galangal (*laos*)	½ tsp, ground
Salam leaf (*daun salam*)	1
Tamarind (*asam Jawa*) juice (see pg 16)	1 Tbsp

Method

- Rub fish all over with salt. Set aside.
- Heat oil and sauté garlic and onion until lightly brown. Add fish and lower heat, then add *sambal oelek*, soy sauce, ginger, galangal and *salam* leaf. Baste repeatedly.
- Cover tightly and cook over very low heat for about 20 minutes. Baste continuously. Water may be added to prevent fish from adhering to pan.
- Add tamarind juice 5 minutes before removing from heat. Serve immediately.

NOTE: This recipe can be used for a large fish such as a 6 kg (13 lb 2 oz) striped bass. Spices, however, must be adjusted according to taste and the size of the catch.

Ikan Bali ❧

(Bali Fish)

Ingredients

Fish	1, about 700–900 g (1 lb 8 oz–2 lb) dressed weight, preferably porgy, sea bass or mackerel
Salt	1 tsp
Cooking oil for deep-frying	
Vegetable oil or margarine	2 Tbsp
Onions	2, small, peeled and sliced
Sambal oelek (see pg 159)	1 tsp
Galangal (*laos*)	½ tsp, ground
Lemon grass (*serai*)	½ tsp, ground
Tamarind (*asam Jawa*) juice (see pg 16)	3 Tbsp
Ginger	a pinch, ground
Brown sugar	1 tsp
Sweet soy sauce (*kecap manis*)	1 Tbsp

Method

- Cut fish into serving portions and rub salt all over. Deep-fry and drain on absorbent paper towels.
- Heat oil or margarine and sauté sliced onions until lightly brown. Add *sambal oelek*, galangal, lemon grass, tamarind juice, ginger, brown sugar and soy sauce. Heat thoroughly.
- Place fried fish in deep serving dish and pour sauce over it. Serve.

Opposite: Ikan Bali

Ikan Panggang ∿

(Barbecue Fish)

Ingredients

Whole fish	1, about 700–900 g (1 lb 8 oz–2 lb) dressed weight, preferably sea bass, bonito or mackerel
Salt	1 tsp
Vegetable oil	4 Tbsp
Water	2 Tbsp
Sweet soy sauce (*kecap manis)*	1 Tbsp
Sambal oelek (see pg 159)	1 tsp

Method

* Slit fish down the backbone. Rub with salt.
* Heat oil in a small saucepan and add water, soy sauce and *sambal oelek*. Stir frequently.
* Roast fish over charcoal heat and baste with cooked liquid mixture until fish is well done. Serve.

Ikan Kari ∿

(Curried Fish)

Ingredients

Whole fish	1, about 700 g (1 lb 8 oz) dressed weight, preferably porgy or sea bass
Salt	1 tsp
Onion	1, large, peeled and sliced
Vegetable oil	2 Tbsp
Garlic	2 cloves, peeled and chopped
Curry powder	2 tsp, or 1 tsp ground turmeric, ½ tsp ground cumin, ½ tsp ground coriander and a pinch of ground ginger combined
Coconut	1 Tbsp, desiccated or freshly grated
Sambal oelek (see pg 159)	1 tsp
Water	250 ml (1 cup)
Tamarind (*asam Jawa*) juice (see pg 16)	1 Tbsp

Method

* Rub fish all over with salt.
* Sauté onion lightly in oil, subsequently adding chopped garlic and curry powder. Stir continuously to prevent curry from burning.
* Add coconut and *sambal oelek*. Fry for about 5 minutes and add water. Bring to the boil.
* Add fish, cover and simmer 15–20 minutes. Finally, add tamarind juice just before serving.

Ikan Teri Goreng ✦

(Fried Anchovies)

Ingredients

Vegetable oil	2 Tbsp
Onion	1, medium, peeled and finely sliced
Sambal oelek (see pg 159)	1 tsp
Anchovy or smelt (fresh or frozen)	450 g (1 lb)
Salt	1½ tsp
Coconut milk	125 ml (½ cup), squeezed from from ½ grated coconut with sufficient water added
Tamarind (*asam Jawa*) juice (see pg 16)	1 Tbsp

Method

- Heat oil in a frying pan (skillet) and sauté onion slices lightly. Add *sambal oelek* and stir.
- Add fish and salt, stirring repeatedly so as to cover fish thoroughly with spices.
- Add coconut milk and tamarind juice, then cover pan and simmer until liquid has been absorbed by fish. Serve warm.

Left: Ikan Teri Goreng

Sambal Goreng Ikan ✦

(Spiced Fish)

Ingredients

Whole fish	1, about 700 g (1 lb 8 oz) dressed weight, preferably porgy, sea bass or gourami
Salt	1½ tsp
Plain (all-purpose) flour	65 g (½ cup)
Cooking oil for deep-frying	
Onion	1, large, peeled and thinly sliced
Vegetable oil	2 Tbsp
Sambal oelek (see pg 159)	1 Tbsp
Tamarind (*asam Jawa*) juice (see pg 16)	1 Tbsp
Water	60 ml (¼ cup)

Method

- Rub fish with 1 tsp salt, then coat with flour. Deep-fry and drain on absorbent paper towels. Keep fish warm.
- Prepare sauce by lightly sautéing sliced onion in oil, then adding *sambal oelek,* tamarind juice, water and remaining salt. Bring to a slow boil, lower heat and simmer for 10 minutes.
- Place fish on a serving dish and pour sauce over it. Serve immediately.

NOTE: Alternatively, use steaks from larger fish, notably cod, haddock or pollock. Everything else follows in the same manner.

Ikan Goreng Asam Manis ✦

(Sweet and Sour Fish)

Ingredients

Whole fish	1, about 450–900 g (1–2 lb), preferably porgy, sea bass or gourami
Salt	1 tsp
Egg	1
Plain (all-purpose) flour	2 Tbsp
Cooking oil for deep-frying	

Sweet and Sour Sauce

Light soy sauce (*kecap asin*)	2 tsp
Corn flour (cornstarch)	3 tsp, mixed with 4 Tbsp water
Tomato sauce (ketchup)	1 Tbsp
Vinegar	60 ml (¼ cup)
Water	125 ml (½ cup)
Sugar	4 Tbsp

Garnishing (optional)

Julienned carrot

Julienned capsicum (bell pepper)

Small pineapple pieces

Thin tomato wedges

Method

- Scale fish with a dull knife and remove the entrails. Wash well. Make two diagonal slits on both sides. Rub prepared fish with salt.
- Mix egg with flour and rub over fish, both inside and out.
- Heat sufficient oil for deep-frying and cook fish until brown. Remove from oil and drain. Place on an oval platter and keep warm.
- Bring all sauce ingredients to the boil, stirring constantly. Pour over fish just before serving.
- Garnish fish with any or all of recommended ingredients. They may be fried lightly before serving.

Begedel Ikan ✑

(Fish Croquettes)

Ingredients

Cod steak or fillet	450 g (1 lb)
Water	500 ml (2 cups)
White bread	2 slices
Eggs	2, yolks and whites separated
Onion	1, small, peeled and finely chopped
Parsley	1 Tbsp, ground
Salt	1 tsp
Breadcrumbs for coating	
Cooking oil for deep-frying	

Method

- Poach fish in water, then flake off flesh in little bits.
- Remove crust from bread and soften in 2 Tbsp water. Gently pull bread apart into small pieces.
- Mix flaked fish with egg yolks, onion, parsley, pieces of bread and salt. Shape mixture into balls about the size of apricots or smaller.
- Beat egg whites until foamy. Dip balls in beaten egg whites, then roll in breadcrumbs.
- Deep-fry breaded balls until medium brown and drain on paper towels. Serve.

NOTE: To make prawn (shrimp) or crab croquettes, simply substitute with chopped raw prawns or crabmeat.

Udang Goreng Asam Manis ✑

(Sweet and Sour Prawns)

Ingredients

Prawns (shrimps)	12, medium-sized
Salt	1 tsp
Egg	1
Plain (all-purpose) flour	2 Tbsp
Cooking oil for deep-frying	

Method

- Peel and devein prawns, then rub with salt.
- Mix egg with flour and dredge prawns in resulting batter.
- Heat sufficient oil for deep-frying and lower in battered prawns to cook.
- Serve cooked prawns with Sweet and Sour Sauce (see Ikan Goreng Asam Manis on pg 38).

Udang Kari ✍

(Prawn Curry)

Ingredients

Vegetable oil	1 Tbsp
Onion	1, medium, peeled and finely chopped
Garlic	2 cloves, peeled and finely chopped
Turmeric (*kunyit*)	1 tsp, ground
Cumin (*jintan*)	½ tsp, ground
Lemon grass (*serai*)	1 tsp, ground
Sambal oelek (see pg 159)	1 tsp
Dried prawn (shrimp) paste (*terasi*)	1 pea-size piece
Salt	1 tsp
Coconut milk	250 ml (1 cup), squeezed from ½ grated coconut with sufficient water added
Prawns (shrimps)	450 g (1 lb), frozen or fresh, peeled, leave tails intact if desired

Method

- Heat oil and lightly sauté onion and garlic.
- Add turmeric, cumin and lemon grass. Stir and add *sambal oelek*, dried prawn paste and salt. Stir again.
- Add coconut milk and bring to the boil. Then, lower heat and add prawns. Simmer uncovered for 15–20 minutes.

Braised Bean Curd with Prawns ✲

Ingredients

Prawns (shrimps)	350 g (³/₄ lb), medium-size, about 20, cleaned and peeled
Spring onion (scallion)	1, minced
Fresh ginger	2 Tbsp, minced
Coriander (*ketumbar*)	½ tsp, ground
Sesame oil	60 ml (¼ cup)
Light soy sauce (*kecap asin*)	125 ml (½ cup)
Firm bean curd	2 pieces
Banana leaf	2 pieces, each 33 x 23 cm (13 x 9 inches)
Bamboo toothpicks or cocktail sticks	
Chicken broth	250 ml (1 cup)
Lemon grass (*serai*)	1 stalk
Salt	to taste
Ground black pepper	to taste

Method

- Chop prawns and combine with spring onion. Mix in half of the following: ginger, coriander, sesame oil and soy sauce. Leave to marinate in the refrigerator for 1 hour.

- Drain bean curd pieces of liquid by wrapping in paper towels. As towels soak through, replace with dry ones. Once bean curd pieces are relatively dry, wrap with new paper towels and put onto a plate. Place a heavy plate on top and leave for 30 minutes; this presses out excess liquid.

- Halve drained bean curd lengthways. With a spoon, gently scoop out a hollow in each half, taking care to leave a good amount along borders and bottom. Reserve removed bean curd for another use.

- Sprinkle bean curd halves with a little sesame oil and soy sauce. Then, fill cavity of one bean curd half with half the prawn mixture. Cover prawn filling with corresponding half. Repeat with remaining halves.

- Wrap each filled bean curd piece with prepared banana leaf, securing with toothpicks or cocktail sticks.

- In a deep frying pan (skillet), combine remaining ginger, coriander, sesame oil and soy sauce, as well as chicken broth and lemon grass. Lower in wrapped bean curd pieces and heat. Cover and simmer for 20 minutes.

- To serve, remove bean curd from banana leaf wrapper and transfer to a serving bowl. Pour braising liquid over, then add salt and pepper to taste. Serve immediately.

Udang Goreng Asam Garam Riau ✲

(Riau Salty and Sour Lobster)

Ingredients

Lobster tails	2, medium
Tamarind (*asam Jawa*) juice (see pg 16)	2 Tbsp
Sweet soy sauce (*kecap manis*)	1 tsp
Salt	½ tsp
Peanut oil or margarine	2 Tbsp

Method

- Scrub lobster shells, split them open from the underside and remove black veins. Slice remaining lobster into portions.

- Mix tamarind juice, soy sauce and salt together. Rub solution into lobster.

- Heat oil in a frying pan (skillet) and fry lobster portions until light brown. Serve hot.

Sambal Goreng Udang ∽

(Spiced Prawns)

Ingredients

Vegetable oil	2 Tbsp
Onion	1, medium, peeled and finely chopped
Garlic	2 cloves, peeled and finely chopped
Candlenuts (*kemiri*)	2, grated
Coriander (*ketumbar*)	1 tsp, ground
Cumin (*jintan*)	a pinch, ground
Turmeric (*kunyit*)	½ tsp, ground
Sambal oelek (see pg 159)	1 tsp
Dried prawn (shrimp) paste (*terasi*)	1 pea-size piece
Prawns (shrimps)	450 g (1 lb), fresh or frozen, peeled
Lemon grass (*serai*)	½ tsp, ground
Coconut milk	125 ml (½ cup), squeezed from ½ grated coconut with sufficient water added
Salam leaves (*daun salam*)	2
Salt	1 tsp

Method

- Heat oil, then lightly sauté onion, garlic, candlenuts, coriander, cumin, turmeric, *sambal oelek* and dried prawn paste.
- Add prawns and lemon grass. Fry lightly.
- Add coconut milk and bring to a slow boil. Lower heat, add *salam* leaves and salt. Simmer uncovered for about 15–20 minutes. Serve.

Sambal Goreng Udang Kering ∽

(Spiced Dry Prawns)

Ingredients

Prawns (shrimps)	450 g (1 lb)
Salt	1 tsp
Vegetable oil	2 Tbsp
Garlic	2 cloves, peeled and finely chopped
Galangal (*laos*)	1 tsp, ground
Lemon grass (*serai*)	½ tsp, ground
Dried prawn (shrimp) paste (*terasi*)	1 pea-size piece
Coconut	1 Tbsp, desiccated or freshly grated
Sambal oelek (see pg 159)	2 tsp

Method

- With shells intact, sprinkle prawns with salt and boil in water. Remove and leave to cool, then peel. Set aside.
- Heat oil and sauté garlic, galangal and lemon grass. Add prawns, dried prawn paste and coconut. Stir continuously and fry until coconut becomes lightly brown.
- Add *sambal oelek* and fry for 5 minutes more. Serve.

Prawns with Garlic and Soy Sauce ⁓

Ingredients

Jumbo prawns (shrimps)	900 g (2 lb), peeled and deveined but with tails intact
Garlic	3 cloves, peeled and chopped
Light soy sauce (*kecap asin*)	1½ Tbsp
Sweet soy sauce (*kecap manis*)	1 Tbsp
Red chilli (optional)	1, thinly sliced
Corn flour (cornstarch)	1 tsp
Cooking oil	3 Tbsp

Method

- Into a bowl, put prawns, garlic, soy sauces, chilli, if used, and corn flour. Mix well.
- Heat oil in a large frying pan (skillet). Add seasoned prawns and sauté over medium heat for about 10 minutes. Take care not to overcook prawns because this toughens them.
- Serve with stir-fried water convolvulus (*kangkung*), if desired. If water convolvulus is unavailable, use watercress.

Udang Pancet Saus Mentega ⁓

(Butterfly Prawns)

Ingredients

Prawns (shrimps)	12, large
Tamarind pulp (*asam Jawa*)	1 Tbsp
Garlic	3 cloves, peeled and chopped
Ginger	1 slice, peeled
Sweet soy sauce (*kecap manis*)	3 Tbsp
Corn flour (cornstarch)	2 tsp
Vegetable oil or margarine	3 Tbsp

Method

- Cut prawns lengthways along the back, but do not remove shells. Remove black vein and wash well.
- Mix prepared prawns with all ingredients except oil.
- Heat oil or margarine and fry prawns for 10–15 minutes.

Opposite: Udang Pancet Saus Mentega

Cumi-cumi Kalimantan ⁓

(Borneo Squid)

Ingredients

Squids	225–450 g (8 oz–1 lb)
Tamarind (*asam Jawa*) juice (see pg 16)	1 Tbsp
Sweet soy sauce (*kecap manis*)	2 Tbsp
Salt	1 tsp
Vegetable oil	2 Tbsp

Method

- Pull off heads of squids and remove ink sacs. Clean squid insides thoroughly, then cut into desired serving portions.
- Rub squid pieces with combined tamarind juice, soy sauce and salt.
- Heat oil in a frying pan (skillet) and add squid. Sauté until done, stirring continuously.

Ikan Braised in Coconut Milk ⁓

Ingredients

Fish fillets	450 g (1 lb), preferably catfish
Salt	
Ground black pepper	
Cinnamon (*kayu manis*)	1 stick, 7.5-cm (3-inches) long
Salam leaves (*daun salam*)	2
Lemon grass (*serai*)	1 stalk, crushed and split
Coriander (*ketumbar*)	2 tsp, ground
Coriander leaves (*cilantro*)	1 sprig
Coconut milk	1 can (400 ml / 131/3 fl oz)
Semi-ripe papaya	1, small, peeled, seeded and julienned

Method

- Wash fish and rub with salt and pepper. Set aside.
- In a frying pan (skillet), combine cinnamon, *salam* leaves, lemon grass, coriander, coriander leaves and coconut milk.
- Add fish to pan, cover tightly and simmer for about 7 minutes or more if fillets are thick.
- Arrange papaya on top of fish, cover tightly again and simmer for about 3 minutes.
- Serve immediately.

Opposite: Cumi-cumi Kalimantan

Bebotok Kepiting Jawa ❧

(Javanese Chopped Crab)

Ingredients

Dried prawn (shrimp) paste (*terasi*)	1 pea-size piece
Coconut milk	125 ml (½ cup), squeezed from 1 grated coconut with sufficient water added
Onion	1, medium, peeled and finely chopped
Garlic	2 cloves, peeled and finely chopped
Candlenuts (*kemiri*)	2, grated
Coriander (*ketumbar*)	1 tsp, ground
Cumin (*jintan*)	a pinch, ground
Turmeric (*kunyit*)	a pinch, ground
Lemon grass (*serai*)	1 stalk
Sambal oelek (see pg 159)	1 tsp
Salt	½ tsp
Eggs	2, lightly beaten
Crabmeat	450 g (1 lb)
Kaffir lime leaf (*daun jeruk purut*)	1, shredded

Method

- Soften dried prawn paste in coconut milk.
- Mix onion, garlic and candlenuts in a deep bowl, then stir in dried prawn paste-coconut milk mixture.
- Add all remaining ingredients except kaffir lime leaf.
- Shape mixture into patties and wrap in aluminium foil, rolling foil so that it is both air-tight and water-tight.
- Put patties into a double-boiler, cover and steam for 1 hour. Add lime leaf after unwrapping foil. Serve warm.

NOTE: A novel serving suggestion is to cook the crab mixture in the top shells instead of using aluminium foil. Both pretty and convenient, as well as easy to handle.

Sop Jagung Telur Kepiting ❧

(Corn and Crab Soup)

Ingredients

Cream corn	1 can (450 g / 1 lb)
Clear chicken broth or water	500 ml (2 cups)
Corn flour (cornstarch)	2 tsp, dissolved in some broth
Light soy sauce (*kecap asin*)	1 tsp
Sugar	½ tsp
Cooked crabmeat	1 cup
Egg white	1, lightly beaten

Method

- Mix cream corn, broth or water, corn flour solution, soy sauce and sugar in a saucepan. Bring to the boil over medium heat, stirring constantly.
- Add crabmeat and return to the boil. Then, turn off heat and stir in egg white. Serve immediately.

NOTE: To add flavour to soup, serve with wine vinegar and soy sauce mixed with red chillies in separate dishes. Each diner adds his own vinegar or spiced soy sauce to taste.

Opposite: Bebotok Kepiting Jawa (top); Sop Jagung Telur Kepiting (bottom)

Poultry

The Asian's fondness for chicken and other dishes made from both domesticated fowl and game-birds rivals that of the average Westerner. However, while chicken has been reduced in the West to everyday or regular fare, replaced by turkey or beef on festive occasions, it remains the fowl of distinction in Asia, rivalled perhaps only by duck. Asian fondness for chicken is not of missile-age vintage. The columinous court records of imperial China, as early as 1000 B.C., tell of farmers raising poultry for meat and eggs. The fact is that today's popular domesticated chickens, the familiar supermarket variety, are Asian in origin — descendants of the red and green jungle-fowls.

Red jungle-fowls, whose wings are brilliant cherry-red, roam the area from Bangladesh and southern China to Malaysia, Java and Sumatra. They are relatively common in scrub country and jungle clearings at low and reasonably moderate altitudes. Green jungle-fowls inhabit Java and the insular stepping stones at the island's eastern tip: Bali, Lombok (where the hottest chillies are grown), Sumbawa, Sumba, Flores and Timor. Bold creatures with bronzy red and green wings, they are often found near rice-fields. They also enjoy the rocky terrain along parts of the craggy coast.

America's internationally celebrated Plymouth Rocks and Rhode Island Reds, for example, share a common Javanese ancestry, as do all other domesticated chickens. In the early 1800s, in the heyday of the Yankee clipper, when the Sumatra spice run was on a commuter basis, returning skippers brought to New England — in addition to spices and recipes acquired in Asian ports — various types of red and green jungle-fowl, some wild, some domesticated. At this juncture, the American farmer took over. By careful selection and cross-breeding, the size, colour, shape and habits of these fowls underwent a radical transformation. Where meat was the objective, poultrymen chose fowls of large size that grew rapidly and cross-bred them until a suitable strain was found; where eggs were the objective, hen-breeding proceeded along similar lines.

It is easy to distinguish between wild and domesticated chickens. The Asian jungle-fowls are thin, have small combs and hold their tails at disdainfully low angles compared to the domesticated types. Jungle-fowls also often have feathered legs. In terms of meat quality, the wild birds are more stringy and tougher than their domesticated counterparts. For that matter, compared to Western chickens, Indonesian domesticated ones are also stringy and on the thin side. The American chicken is too plump, so fulsome as to be tasteless and bland. Curiously, a tough, scrawny chicken may be a challenge to the cook but the bird is actually tastier than a plump chicken when prepared in the highly spiced Indonesian style. I sometimes suspect that the meat of stringy, gamy Asian birds is better able to absorb marinating and basting sauces than that of the pampered scientifically raised Western strains.

In the twenty-first century, the mass-produced chickens in the U.S. might be inexpensive but they no longer have the taste or consistency of what I consider *real* chickens. Be aware that mass-produced chickens have a much higher water and fat content and they easily break down in the pot. It is better to buy the best-quality chickens, which can be more pricey. You might pay more upfront but you will end up with more meat and less liquid. It is well worth the extra cost.

The best chickens for Indonesian recipes are fryers or broilers (as they are called in the U.S.). These are tender, young, active birds, usually 10–16 weeks old. They have a small amount of fat and soft bones. In weight, they average 450 g–1.35 kg (1–3 lb). For the recipes here, use chickens about 1.15 kg (2 lb 8 oz) in weight. Cooked in spices, sweet soy or coconut milk, they provide a welcome twist in cooking an old favourite. Indeed, Indonesians, as the rice table testifies, prefer many twists. In Indonesia, a chicken is often quartered and then cooked four different ways to add still more variety to the meal.

This emphasis on cooking chicken is somewhat misleading. In addition to chicken, Indonesia and neighbouring Asia abound in duck and game-birds such as jungle partridge, quail and pheasant. A tip to hunters: a game-bird may be substituted for chicken in these spicy Indonesian recipes. The result is a superb, unforgettable dish that borders on sensational. I have eliminated them from these recipes since game-birds are not commercially available to the average home cook. Cornish hens are too small, although they are sometimes reminiscent of Indonesian chickens.

The ducks of Indonesia, by the way, are similar to those found on Long Island — fat and succulent. The islands are well stocked with mallard, teal and pintail. Here, as elsewhere in Asia, the Chinese must be credited with cooking them in the most delectable manner; Sino-Indonesian restaurants, in this regard, are perhaps unrivalled except for fabled Peking or Beijing (but not having been there, I do not really know). In the highlands around Bandung, the mountain capital of western Java, turkeys are raised for the handful of foreigners in residence in Jakarta. However, in Southeast Asia, the best turkeys are the frozen Australian birds readily available at Singapore supermarkets; when we lived in Indonesia, visiting foreign correspondents often brought turkeys as gifts. One American Thanksgiving Day, there was a disaster. George Rice and the late Peter Gruening of United Press arrived with a bird. I rushed to our village *pasar* (market) for some berries and was horrified when I returned. Roemina, my kitchen helper, to be helpful, had diced the big bird in true Indonesian style! So much for visions of roast turkey in a tropical setting.

Before delving into the poultry dishes, a final note: in the preparation of Nasi Goreng or Indonesian fried rice, leftover chicken, duck and turkey may be used with abandon; indeed, leftovers are encouraged. In our household, within a week of a national holiday, such as Thanksgiving, members of my hungry household are whetting their appetites for Nasi Goreng *à la* turkey.

Ayam Kecap ✑

(Soy Chicken)

Ingredients

Chicken (broiler/fryer)	1, about 1.15 kg (2 lb 8 oz)
Salt	2 tsp
Vegetable oil	3 Tbsp
Onion	1, medium, peeled and finely chopped
Nutmeg (*pala*)	a pinch, grated
Sweet soy sauce (*kecap manis*)	3 Tbsp
Tamarind (*asam Jawa*) juice (see pg 16)	½ tsp
Water	250 ml (1 cup)

Method

- Cut chicken into desired serving portions and rub thoroughly with salt.
- Heat oil in a large, heavy frying pan (skillet) with a tight-fitting cover. Then, add chicken and fry until light brown, stirring frequently to prevent it from sticking to the pan.
- Add onion and stir to combine with chicken. Fry until onion turns mellow brown.
- Add all remaining ingredients and stir well, frying mixture for about 20 minutes.
- Add water, cover and simmer over low heat for 20–30 minutes. Serve.

Ayam O ✑

(Chicken O)

Ingredients

Chicken (broiler/fryer)	1, about 1.15 kg (2 lb 8 oz)
Salt	2 tsp
Ground black pepper	½ tsp
Vegetable oil or margarine	3 Tbsp
Garlic	3 cloves, peeled and finely chopped
Ginger	a pinch, ground
Brown sugar	1 tsp
Dried prawn (shrimp) paste (*terasi*)	1 pea-size piece, dissolved in 2 Tbsp water
Spring onions (scallions)	2, chopped
Sweet soy sauce (*kecap manis*)	2 Tbsp

Method

- Cut chicken into serving portions. Wash thoroughly and drain. Rub thoroughly with salt and pepper, then let stand for about 10 minutes.
- Heat oil or margarine in a frying pan (skillet). Add chicken followed by garlic. Fry until light brown.
- Add ginger and brown sugar and stir. Add dissolved prawn paste and stir well again. Fry for about 2 minutes.
- Mix in spring onions and soy sauce. Cover mixture, reduce heat and cook for about 30 minutes. Add a little water if necessary to prevent drying. Serve.

Opposite: Ayam O

Ayam Kuning ❧
(Yellow Chicken)

Ingredients

Chicken (broiler/fryer)	1, about 1.15 kg (2 lb 8 oz)
Coriander (*ketumbar*)	½ tsp, ground
Galangal (*laos*)	½ tsp, ground
Salt	2 tsp
Vegetable oil	3 Tbsp
Turmeric (*kunyit*)	1½ tsp, ground
Onion	1, medium, peeled and thinly sliced
Garlic	2 cloves, peeled and chopped
Candlenuts (*kemiri*)	2, grated
Lemon grass (*serai*)	a pinch, ground
Coconut milk	500 ml (2 cups), squeezed from 1 grated coconut with sufficient water added
Tamarind (*asam Jawa*) juice (see pg 16)	1 Tbsp

Method

- Cut chicken into serving portions. Rub thoroughly with a mixture of coriander, galangal and salt.
- Fry chicken in oil until medium brown. Add turmeric and stir-fry 2 minutes more.
- Add onion and garlic and fry for 1 minute. Then, add candlenuts and lemon grass. Stir-fry well.
- Finally, add coconut milk and tamarind juice. Simmer over low heat for 30–45 minutes. Serve.

Ayam Besengek ⁓

(Chicken Besengek)

Ingredients

Chicken (broiler/fryer)	1, about 1.15 kg (2 lb 8 oz)
Salt	2 tsp
Vegetable oil	3 Tbsp
Onions	2, medium, peeled and finely chopped
Garlic	2 cloves, peeled and finely chopped
Red chillies	2, crushed
Coriander (*ketumbar*)	1 tsp, ground
Cumin (*jintan*)	a pinch, ground
Galangal (*laos*)	1 tsp, ground
Candlenuts (*kemiri*)	2, grated
Dried prawn (shrimp) paste (*terasi*)	½ tsp
Coconut	2 Tbsp, desiccated or freshly grated
Coconut milk	500 ml (2 cups), squeezed from 1 grated coconut with sufficient water added
Brown sugar	1 tsp
Tamarind (*asam Jawa*) juice (see pg 16)	1 Tbsp

Method

- Cut chicken into serving portions and rub with salt. Then, fry in oil until light brown.
- Add onions and garlic and stir-fry until onions turn medium brown.
- Add chillies, coriander, cumin and galangal. Stir-fry for about 1 minute.
- Add candlenuts to mixture and stir well. Add dried prawn paste and grated coconut. Stir-fry for 1 minute more.
- Add coconut milk and brown sugar. Simmer over low heat for about 30 minutes. Finally, add in tamarind juice. Serve.

Ayam Panggang Sumatra ⁓

(Sumatran Barbecue Chicken)

Ingredients

Chicken (broiler/fryer)	1, small, about 1 kg (2 lb 3 oz)
Sweet soy sauce (*kecap manis*)	2 Tbsp
Tamarind (*asam Jawa*) juice (see pg 16)	2 Tbsp
Butter or margarine	3 Tbsp
Salt	1 tsp
Red chillies	3, crushed

Method

- Quarter chicken and parboil for 10 minutes. Drain.
- In a saucepan, heat soy sauce, tamarind juice, butter or margarine and salt over low heat. Remove as soon as butter or margarine melts. Add in crushed chillies and mix well.
- Marinate chicken pieces in spicy mixture for 15 minutes.
- Broil (grill) over red-hot, smokeless charcoal heat, basting frequently with mixture. Serve hot.

Rempah Ayam

(Spiced Chicken Cakes)

Ingredients

Chicken breast	1, large, about 450 g (1 lb)
White bread	1 slice
Garlic	1 clove, peeled and chopped
Onion	1, small, peeled and chopped
Red chilli	¼, crushed
Coriander (*ketumbar*)	1 tsp, ground
Cumin (*jintan*)	a pinch, ground
Coconut	2 Tbsp, desiccated or freshly grated
Egg	1, lightly beaten
Dried prawn (shrimp) paste (*terasi*)	1 pea-size piece
Salt	1 tsp
Breadcrumbs	
Vegetable oil	

Method

- Remove chicken meat from breast bone and chop finely. Set aside.
- Remove crust from bread. Crumble bread into small pieces. Mix chicken and bread in a bowl.
- Combine garlic and onion with chicken mixture. Then, add chilli, coriander, cumin, coconut, egg, dried prawn paste and salt. Mix thoroughly.
- Shape into small patties, sprinkle with breadcrumbs and fry on both sides in oil until medium brown. Serve.

Ayam Smor ❧
(Braised Chicken)

Ingredients

Chicken (broiler/fryer)	1, about 1.35 kg (3 lb)
Salt	2 tsp
Vegetable oil	3 Tbsp
Onion	1, large, peeled and sliced
Garlic	2 cloves, peeled and chopped
Chopped ginger	a pinch
Nutmeg (*pala*)	a pinch, grated
Coriander (*ketumbar*)	1 tsp, ground
Ground black pepper	½ tsp
Dried prawn (shrimp) paste (*terasi*)	1 pea-size piece
Light soy sauce (*kecap asin*)	1 tsp
Water	250 ml (1 cup)
Tamarind (*asam Jawa*) juice (see pg 16)	1 Tbsp

Method

- Cut chicken into serving portions and rub with salt. Fry pieces in vegetable oil until light brown.
- Add onion and garlic, frying until onion turns light brown.
- Add ginger, nutmeg, coriander, black pepper, dried prawn paste and soy sauce. Fry for about 1 minute.
- Add water and tamarind juice. Cover tightly and simmer over low heat until chicken is tender. Serve.

Ayam Pekalongan ❧
(Pekalongan Chicken)

A favourite dish in central Java. It derives its name from Pekalongan, a sleepy, dusty Javanese town near the southern coast of the island.

Ingredients

Chicken (broiler/fryer)	1, about 1.15 kg (2 lb 8 oz)
Vegetable oil	2 Tbsp
Onion	1, large, peeled and finely chopped
Garlic	2 cloves, peeled and finely chopped
Galangal (*laos*)	1 tsp, ground
Red chilli	1, crushed
Dried prawn (shrimp) paste (*terasi*)	1 pea-size piece
Salt	2 tsp
Tamarind (*asam Jawa*) juice (see pg 16)	3 Tbsp
Coconut milk	125 ml (½ cup), squeezed from ½ grated coconut with sufficient water added

Method

- Put chicken into a large saucepan. Add sufficient water to cover chicken, then simmer until tender.
- Remove chicken from stock. Leave to cool and debone. Dice chicken meat. Set aside.
- Heat oil in a heavy frying pan (skillet). Fry onion and garlic until light brown.
- Add galangal and chilli. Stir well, then add chicken, dried prawn paste and salt. Fry chicken until almost dry, stirring frequently.
- Add tamarind juice and coconut milk. Cover and cook until stock is almost completely absorbed by chicken.
- Serve garnished with red chilli strips, if desired.

Opposite: Ayam Pekalongan

Opor Ayam ৵৶

(Chicken in Coconut)

Ingredients

Chicken (broiler/fryer)	1, about 1.15 kg (2 lb 8 oz)
Salt	2 tsp
Onion	1, large, peeled and finely chopped
Garlic	3 cloves, peeled and finely chopped
Vegetable oil	3 Tbsp
Coriander (*ketumbar*)	1 Tbsp, ground
Chopped ginger	a pinch
Lemon grass (*serai*)	1 tsp, ground
Coconut milk	500 ml (2 cups), squeezed from 1 grated coconut with sufficient water added
Salam leaf (*daun salam*)	1

Method

- Cut chicken into serving portions and rub with salt.
- Fry onion and garlic in vegetable oil until light brown. Then, add coriander, ginger and lemon grass. Stir well and fry for about 1 minute.
- Add chicken, mixing thoroughly so that chicken absorbs the spices.
- Add coconut milk and *salam* leaf. Cover tightly and cook over medium heat for about 40 minutes. Serve.

Ayam Abon-abon ৵৶

(Shredded Chicken)

Ingredients

Chicken breast	1, large, about 450 g (1 lb)
Coriander (*ketumbar*)	½ tsp, ground
Galangal (*laos*)	½ tsp, ground
Tamarind (*asam Jawa*) juice (see pg 16)	2 Tbsp
Salt	1 tsp
Vegetable oil	2 Tbsp

Method

- Put chicken breast into a saucepan, add sufficient water to cover and cook for 20 minutes until tender.
- Remove chicken from stock. Leave to cool and shred meat from breast bone. Set aside.
- Put shredded chicken into bowl. Add coriander, galangal, tamarind juice and salt. Mix thoroughly.
- Fry seasoned chicken in vegetable oil in a heavy frying pan (skillet), stirring frequently until meat is dry and crisp. Serve as a *rijsttafel* garnish.

Opposite: Ayam Abon-abon

Ayam Ternate ✌

(Ternate Chicken)

Although this dish is popular on fabulous Ternate, it conspicuously omits the spice that made Ternate famous and drew rival Dutch, Portuguese and Spanish merchants in the sixteenth century — nutmeg. For a short time, Ternate rivalled Banda as the world's primary source of nutmeg and mace (the outer covering of nutmeg).

Ingredients

Chicken (broiler/fryer)	1, about 1.15 kg (2 lb 8 oz)
Ginger	a pinch, ground
Lemon grass (*serai*)	1 tsp, ground
Candlenuts (*kemiri*)	3, grated
Salt	2 tsp
Vegetable oil	3 Tbsp
Onion	1, large, peeled and sliced
Garlic	3 cloves, peeled and chopped
Red chilli	1, crushed
Dried prawn (shrimp) paste (*terasi*)	1 pea-size piece
Tamarind (*asam Jawa*) juice (see pg 16)	2 Tbsp
Kaffir lime leaves (*daun jeruk purut*)	3
Coconut milk	250 ml (1 cup), squeezed from ½ grated coconut with sufficient water added

Method

- Cut chicken into small pieces. Set aside.
- Mix together ginger, lemon grass, candlenuts and salt. Rub chicken with this spice mixture.
- Fry seasoned chicken pieces in oil until golden brown. Then, add onion and garlic and fry until onion turns light brown.
- Add chilli, dried prawn paste, tamarind juice and lime leaves. Fry for 1 minute more, stirring constantly.
- Add coconut milk and cook, uncovered, over low heat until liquid is almost completely evaporated or absorbed. Serve.

Ayam Bumbu Rujak ✌

(Chicken in Pungent Sauce)

Ingredients

Chicken (broiler/fryer)	1, about 1.15 kg (2 lb 8 oz)
Onion	1, large, peeled and finely chopped
Garlic	2 cloves, peeled and finely chopped
Vegetable oil	3 Tbsp
Brown sugar	1 tsp
Red chilli	1, crushed
Candlenuts (*kemiri*)	2, grated
Dried prawn (shrimp) paste (*terasi*)	1 pea-size piece
Tamarind (*asam Jawa*) juice (see pg 16)	1 Tbsp
Sweet soy sauce (*kecap manis*)	1 tsp
Water	250 ml (1 cup)
Salt	2 tsp

Method

- Cut chicken into serving portions. Set aside.
- Fry onion and garlic in oil until golden brown. Then, add brown sugar, chilli, candlenuts and dried prawn paste. Stir to combine.
- Add chicken to spice mixture. Then, add all remaining ingredients and cover tightly. Allow to cook slowly until liquid is completely absorbed by chicken. Serve.

Ayam Bawang ✐
(Chicken with Onions)

Ingredients

Chicken (broiler/fryer)	1, about 1.35 kg (3 lb)
Salt	3 tsp
Ground black pepper	½ tsp
Vegetable oil or margarine	3 Tbsp
Garlic	3 cloves, peeled and crushed
Chopped ginger	a pinch
Galangal (*laos*)	1 tsp, ground
Red chilli	½, crushed
Tamarind (*asam Jawa*) juice (see pg 16)	2 Tbsp
Sweet soy sauce (*kecap manis*)	1 Tbsp
Water	250 ml (1 cup)
White onions	10, small, peeled

Method

- Cut chicken into serving portions. Rub thoroughly with salt and black pepper.
- Fry chicken pieces in oil or margarine until medium brown.
- Add garlic, ginger and galangal. Stir-fry for about 1 minute.
- Add chilli, tamarind juice and soy sauce. While stirring, add water and whole onions. Cover and simmer over low heat for about 30 minutes. Serve.

Burung Darah Goreng ✐
(Fried Pigeon)

Ingredients

Pigeons	2
Honey	2 Tbsp
Light soy sauce (*kecap asin*)	3 Tbsp
Garlic	2 cloves, peeled and crushed
Salt	½ tsp
Cooking oil for deep-frying	
Lettuce for garnishing	

Method

- Wash pigeons well, then rub in- and outside with mixture of honey, soy sauce, garlic and salt.
- Heat sufficient oil for deep-frying and lower in seasoned pigeons to cook until brown. Drain.
- Cut pigeons into small pieces and serve hot on a bed of lettuce.
- To make a perfect accompanying dip, mix equal amounts of salt and freshly ground black pepper.

NOTE: This dish may be made equally well with chicken.

Soto Ayam ❧

(Spicy Chicken Stew)

Ingredients

Chicken (broiler/fryer)	1, small, about 1 kg (2 lb 3 oz)
Water	1 litre (4 cups)
Salt	3 tsp
Vegetable oil	3 Tbsp, for shallow-frying
Onion	1, large, peeled and thinly sliced
Vegetable oil or margarine	1 Tbsp
Garlic	2 cloves, peeled and chopped
Black peppercorns	5
Turmeric (*kunyit*)	a pinch, ground
Chopped ginger	a pinch
Thin egg or transparent (glass) noodles	120 g (4 oz)
Spring onion (scallion)	1, both bulb and shoot, finely chopped
Bean sprouts	1 cup, washed and cleaned

Method

- Cut chicken into small portions and put into a heavy frying pan (skillet). Add water and salt, then cover and cook over low heat until chicken is tender.
- Remove chicken from stock and reserve stock for later use. Let chicken cool, then debone and fry in oil until brown. Set aside.
- Fry onion in oil or margarine until deep brown. Remove from pan and set aside.
- In the same pan, fry garlic, peppercorns, turmeric and ginger for about 2 minutes. Pour this mixture into chicken stock. Bring to a slow boil.
- Lower noodles into boiling chicken stock. Reduce heat to simmer.
- Add spring onion to stock, simmering over low heat for 5–8 minutes.
- Put some bean sprouts and chicken into serving bowls, then ladle soup over. Sprinkle with fried shallot slices and serve.

Ayam Kari Jawa ✥
(Javanese Curried Chicken)

Ingredients

Chicken (broiler/fryer)	1, about 1.15 kg (2 lb 8 oz)
Salt	2 tsp
Vegetable oil	3 Tbsp
Onion	1, large, peeled and chopped
Garlic	3 cloves, peeled and chopped
Turmeric (*kunyit*)	1½ tsp, ground
Coriander (*ketumbar*)	1 tsp, ground
Cumin (*jintan*)	½ tsp, ground
Galangal (*laos*)	1 tsp, ground
Lemon grass (*serai*)	½ tsp, ground
Red chilli	1, crushed
Coconut milk	250 ml (1 cup), squeezed from ½ grated coconut with sufficient water added

Method

- Cut chicken into small portions and rub thoroughly with salt.
- In a frying pan (skillet), fry chicken in vegetable oil until golden brown. Remove chicken.
- In the same pan, fry onion and garlic until medium brown.
- Add combined turmeric, coriander and cumin. Fry for 1 minute, stirring continuously. Then, add galangal, lemon grass and chilli.
- Return chicken to pan and mix thoroughly with spice mixture. Add coconut milk and cook, uncovered, until chicken is tender. Serve.

Ayam Goreng Rempah ✥
(Spicy Fried Chicken)

Ingredients

Chicken (broiler/fryer)	1, about 1.35 kg (3 lb)
Garlic	2 cloves, peeled and finely chopped
Ground black pepper	1 tsp
Lemon grass (*serai*)	1 tsp, ground
Coriander (*ketumbar*)	1 tsp, ground
Dried prawn (shrimp) paste (*terasi*)	1 pea-size piece
Light soy sauce (*kecap asin*)	1 tsp
Tamarind (*asam Jawa*) juice (see pg 16)	1 Tbsp
Salt	2 tsp
Vegetable oil	3 Tbsp

Method

- Cut chicken into small pieces. Set aside.
- In a mixing bowl, combine garlic, pepper, lemon grass, coriander, dried prawn paste, soy sauce, tamarind juice and salt. Mix in chicken and leave to season for at least 30 minutes.
- Heat oil in a heavy frying pan (skillet), then fry seasoned chicken, uncovered, until deep golden brown. Stir constantly so that chicken does not stick to the pan. If necessary, a small amount of water may be used for this purpose. Serve immediately.

Opposite: Ayam Goreng Rempah

Bebek Panggang ⬳

(Barbecue Duck)

Ingredients

Duckling	1, about 1.35 kg (3 lb)
Salt	1 tsp
Water	250 ml (1 cup)

Barbecue Sauce

Sweet soy sauce (*kecap manis*)	3 Tbsp
Tamarind (*asam Jawa*) juice (see pg 16)	2 Tbsp
Red chilli	½ or more to taste, crushed
Vegetable oil	2 Tbsp
Salt	1 tsp

Method

- Quarter cleaned ducking and put pieces into a heavy saucepan. Add 1 tsp salt and water. Cook over low heat for about 20 minutes. Remove duckling from stock and set aside.
- Combine all barbecue sauce ingredients in a bowl. Baste duckling pieces with this sauce and broil (grill) them over red-hot, smokeless charcoal.
- Baste frequently. Cook until duckling pieces are crisp and brown. Serve.

Ayam Makassar ⬳

(Macassar Chicken)

Ingredients

Chicken breasts	2, about 450 g (1 lb) each
Coriander (*ketumbar*)	1½ tsp, ground
Cumin (*jintan*)	a pinch, ground
Ground black pepper	½ tsp
Coconut	3 Tbsp, desiccated or freshly grated
Vegetable oil	3 Tbsp
Coconut milk	250 ml (1 cup), squeezed from ¼ grated coconut with sufficient water added
Lemon grass (*serai*)	1 tsp, ground
Kaffir lime leaves (*daun jeruk purut*)	3
Salt	1 tsp

Method

- Remove chicken meat from breast bone and chop into fine pieces. Set aside.
- Sauté coriander, cumin, black pepper and grated coconut in vegetable oil until coconut starts to brown.
- Add chicken meat and stir-fry well before adding all remaining ingredients. Cook, uncovered, until almost dry, stirring continuously. Serve.

Opposite: Ayam Makassar

Bebek Smor Kecap ✦

(Braised Soy Duck)

Ingredients

Duckling	1, about 1.35 kg (3 lb)
Honey or brown sugar	2 Tbsp
Light soy sauce (*kecap asin*)	125 ml (½ cup)
Star anise (*bunga lawang*)	1 piece, or 1 stick cinnamon (*kayu manis*), 5-cm (2-inches) long
Ginger	1 slice, peeled
Garlic	3 cloves, peeled

Method

- Put all ingredients into a large pot. Cook over medium heat until duckling is tender.
- Cut cooked duckling into serving portions and arrange on an oval serving dish. Transfer remaining gravy to a separate dish. Serve.

NOTE: If ground ginger is used, do use it sparingly.

Bebek Smor ✦

(Braised Duck)

Ingredients

Duckling	1, about 1.35 kg (3 lb)
Salt	3 tsp
Water	750 ml (3 cups)
Vegetable oil	2 Tbsp
Onions	2, medium, peeled and finely chopped
Garlic	2 cloves, peeled and finely chopped
Coriander (*ketumbar*)	1 tsp, ground
Candlenuts (*kemiri*)	2, grated
Salam leaves (*daun salam*)	2
Dried prawn (shrimp) paste (*terasi*)	1 pea-size piece
Lemon	½, both juice and rind

Method

- Cut duckling into serving portions, then transfer to a large saucepan. Add salt and water and cook over low heat until tender. Remove duckling pieces from stock and set aside.
- Heat oil in a frying pan (skillet). Fry onions and garlic until mellow brown. Add coriander and candlenuts. Mix thoroughly.
- Finally, add duckling pieces together with *salam* leaves, dried prawn paste and lemon juice and rind. Cook, covered, over very low heat until liquid is almost entirely absorbed. Serve.

Opposite: Bebek Smor Kecap

Meat

In Indonesia, the cooking of beef has evolved into a fine art. A hallmark of Indonesian beef dishes is the art of marinating. No festive rice table is complete without beef and it usually appears in several forms — shredded, dried, steamed or curried. For the most part, however, Indonesian beef is stringy, tough and gamy. Choice cuts are different from those in the West and frequently, there is little choice of cuts. Beef, moreover, is expensive on the islands and is, therefore, used sparingly. It is prepared with as little waste as possible.

The main sources of domesticated cattle are slate-coloured water-buffalo, a sluggish draught animal which delights in wallowing in water and mud, and the ubiquitous hump-backed white Brahmin steer which does double duty hauling a bullock cart. Since these animals are comparable to tractors, they represent a heavy capital investment and are social status symbols on par with the Mercedes-Benz-cum-mink syndrome in the West and are apt to avoid an early trip to the slaughterhouse. Herds of buffalo crossing roads and highways, nevertheless, are common sights and the casualty rate is reasonably high — and so is the number of unexpected feasts in villages contiguous to the main traffic arteries.

The more popular methods of preparing beef in Indonesia are sautéing, braising, fricasseeing and frying with aromatic, pungent and searing spices, particularly cinnamon, nutmeg, coriander and crushed red chilli. In Indonesia, sautéing involves the browning of slivers of meat and spices in a heavy frying pan lightly greased with margarine or coconut or peanut oil. In braising and fricasseeing, slivers or cubes of meat that have already been sautéed are cooked in a covered saucepan or stewed in a thick liquid together with vegetables and additional spices. In Indonesian frying, as in the West, the cooking of the meat is done in an inch or two of vegetable oil or margarine.

Argentine, American or Australian beef by itself is superb: they are the 'Three As' of the beef world. Prepared in the Indonesian style, the beef acquires added luster. Any fine-grained, firm and lean American beef is suitable for the rice table; my own preferences are for either boneless, top sirloin or topside (top round). I use minute steaks in the preparation of *satay* or skewered meat.

Beef, of course, is not the only meat consumed with gusto in Indonesia. Goat is also popular as are lamb and mutton. Here again 'Three As' lamb and mutton are of superior quality and ideally suited in the dishes that follow.

In one respect, however, Indonesia presents a somewhat startling picture on the meat sector. Indonesia, with the exception of Malaysia, is probably the only Muslim country in the world where large quantities of pork are consumed. The Indonesian Muslims, who constitute about ninety per cent of the population, will not touch pork (quite literally), but on Hindu Bali, in the Christian areas of Sumatra, Sulawesi, Maluku and the Lesser Sundas, and among the Sino-European-influenced communities in the bigger cities, pork is widely sold. The islands themselves abound with wild swine. These tusked beasts are as dangerous as they are brave and often raid *padi* fields close to villages. They are also meat eaters and have been known to take on pythons. Pig hunts are common in western Java and southeastern Sumatra, where the swine hide in forests of teak and in the swampy jungle interior (Indonesian swine are good swimmers, likewise Indonesian tigers).

On Bali, pig-raising is commercially profitable and pigs going to market in bamboo baskets are daily sights — their destinations: Singapore, and Chinese shops in Kalimantan and peninsular Malaysia. The Balinese pig, I can testify, is among the world's finest. On one of our trips to Bali, a close group of friends from Ubud presented us with a surprise departure gift at the airfield — a *babi berguling* or suckling pig roasted over a spit and basted, Balinese style, with a spicy marinade. From Bali we flew home to Java with visions of a sumptuous feast in the making.

Over the years, pork in the U.S. has grown leaner and leaner. It is now touted as "the other white meat" to make it sound more like the presumably healthier chicken. The consequence of pork without its traditional fat content is that it dries out very quickly when cooked in older recipes. You can do two things: cook pork for less time and/or brine the pork before cooking.

Previously, pork would carry trichina, small worms that are parasites and cause trichinosis. That is why pork was cooked so long — the lengthy cooking process killed the parasite. Today, commercially raised pigs do not have the same risks, so cooking times can be reduced.

As for brining pork before cooking, I don't necessarily brine all my pork but sometimes I find that putting the pork for 1-2 hours (or even overnight in the refrigerator) in a brine bath consisting of about ½ cup sea salt and 750-1000 ml (3-4 cups) water, adds a tremendous amount of flavour and juiciness. Because commercially raised pigs are so much leaner today, much of the flavour has also been reduced. Of course, today, a new type of pork is being touted as "heritage" pork and some small farmers in the U.S. are producing, in very small amounts, old-fashioned fatty pork that is very, very tasty (and pricey).

As you will quickly observe in the next few pages, the beef and pork recipes are strongly suggestive of Chinese influence, particularly in the fine slicing or dicing of the meat. There is also a distinct Indian or Pakistani touch in the curried dishes, although it should be stressed that Indonesian curry is unlike the curry found on the subcontinent. The addition of Indonesian spices and techniques have transported these Sino-Indian-style dishes to new heights.

DENDENG *Dendeng* is a popular style of meat preservation in Indonesia. The meat is invariably sliced thinly, rubbed with spices, herbs and salt and set out to dry in the sun. It can be kept almost indefinitely. Indonesians prepare *dendeng*, in order of popularity, from venison, buffalo, beef, and beef liver. This mode of preservation may be characterised as spicy, dry refrigeration. It probably was extremely popular in medieval Europe and the need for spices motivated the later voyages of discovery. Obviously, the method has no place in the modern kitchen, but it remains a superb type of food even when freshly prepared. *Dendeng* is simple to prepare, and a must.

Dendeng Manis ✦
(Sweet Dried Beef)

Ingredients

Beef topside (top round)	450 g (1 lb)
Coriander (*ketumbar*)	1 tsp, ground
Cumin (*jintan*)	a pinch, ground
Galangal (*laos*)	1 tsp, ground
Nutmeg (*pala*)	½ tsp, grated
Brown sugar	1 Tbsp
Salt	1 tsp
Vegetable oil	2 Tbsp
Onion	1, peeled and chopped
Garlic	1 clove, peeled and chopped
Dried prawn (shrimp) paste (*terasi*)	1 pea-size piece
Tamarind (*asam Jawa*) juice (see pg 16)	1 tsp
Water	375 ml (1½ cups)

Method

- Slice beef into thin strips. Season meat with a mixture of coriander, cumin, galangal, nutmeg, brown sugar and salt.
- Heat oil in a frying pan (skillet) and add meat, frying until medium brown.
- Add onion and garlic and fry for about 1 minute, then add dried prawn paste, tamarind juice and water. Cover and simmer until completely dry. Serve.

Dendeng Santan ✦
(Coconut Dried Beef)

Ingredients

Beef topside (top round)	450 g (1 lb)
Garlic	2 cloves, peeled and finely chopped
Candlenuts (*kemiri*)	2, grated
Coriander (*ketumbar*)	½ tsp, ground
Tamarind (*asam Jawa*) juice (see pg 16)	1 Tbsp
Brown sugar	1 tsp
Galangal (*laos*)	1 tsp, ground
Salt	1 tsp
Dried prawn (shrimp) paste (*terasi*)	2 pea-size pieces
Coconut milk	125 ml (½ cup), squeezed from ½ grated coconut with sufficient water added
Vegetable oil	2 Tbsp

Method

- Cut beef into slender slices. Rub meat first with garlic and candlenuts, then coriander, tamarind juice, brown sugar, galangal and salt. Set aside.
- Dissolve dried prawn paste in a little coconut milk.
- Heat oil in a frying pan (skillet) and fry meat until it turns a medium brown. Then, add dried prawn paste, cover and cook until almost dry.
- The final touch: add remaining coconut milk and stir well. Cover and cook again until dry.
- Serve garnish with red chilli slices, if desired.

Opposite: Dendeng Santan

Rendang Padang ⮂

(Padang Beef)

Ingredients

Vegetable oil	1 Tbsp
Garlic	2 cloves, peeled and finely chopped
Turmeric (*kunyit*)	1 tsp, ground
Ginger	½ tsp, ground
Lemon grass (*serai*)	½ stalk
Beef topside (top round)	450 g (1 lb), or lean beef, thinly sliced
Red chillies	2 or more to taste, crushed
Salt	1 tsp or more to taste
Coconut milk	375 ml (1½ cups), squeezed from 1 grated coconut with sufficient water added
Salam leaf (*daun salam*)	1

Method

- Heat oil in a frying pan (skillet). Add garlic, turmeric, ginger and lemon grass. Sauté lightly.
- Add meat and crushed chillies. Sauté for 3 minutes, stirring frequently. Add salt and mix well.
- Pour coconut milk over meat and add *salam* leaf. Cover and cook over low heat until almost dry. Serve.

Begedel Cabe ⮂

(Peppered Beef Croquettes)

Ingredients

Minced (ground) beef	225 g (7½ oz)
Egg	2, yolks and whites separated
Garlic	1 clove, peeled and finely chopped
Spring onion (scallion)	1, finely chopped
Parsley	1 Tbsp, chopped
Lemon grass (*serai*)	1 tsp, ground
Ginger	a pinch, ground
Coriander (*ketumbar*)	1 tsp, ground
Salt	1 tsp
Red chillies	12
Breadcrumbs	
Vegetable oil for deep-frying	

Method

- Knead beef with egg yolks, then with garlic and spring onion.
- Add in parsley, lemon grass, ginger, coriander and salt. Mix well and set aside.
- Slit chillies lengthways, remove seeds and stuff with beef mixture. Set aside.
- Beat egg whites until foamy and coat top of beef. Sprinkle with breadcrumbs, then deep-fry. Drain on absorbent paper towels. Serve.

Opposite: Rendang Padang

Gulai Koja
(Dried Curried Beef)

Ingredients

Beef topside (top round)	450 g (1 lb)
Tamarind (*asam Jawa*) juice (see pg 16)	1 tsp
Salt	1 tsp
Rice flour	1 tsp
Turmeric (*kunyit*)	½ tsp, ground
Cloves (*cengkeh*)	a pinch, ground
Cumin (*jintan*)	a pinch, ground
Ginger	a pinch, ground
Coriander (*ketumbar*)	1 tsp, ground
Vegetable oil	2 Tbsp
Garlic	1 clove, peeled and chopped
Onions	5, small, peeled and thinly sliced
Mace (*sekar pala*)	2 pieces
Cinnamon (*kayu manis*)	1 stick, 5-cm (2-inches) long
Coconut milk	375 ml (1½ cups), squeezed from 1 grated coconut with sufficient water added

Method

- Cut beef into thin slices and rub thoroughly with tamarind juice and salt. Set aside.
- In a bowl, mix rice flour with turmeric, cloves, cumin, ginger and coriander. Set spice mixture aside.
- Heat oil and sauté meat and garlic lightly. Then, add onions and sauté until golden brown.
- Pour spice mixture over meat and mix well, frying for about 1 minute.
- Add mace, cinnamon stick and coconut milk. Cover and cook over low heat until meat is almost dry. Serve.

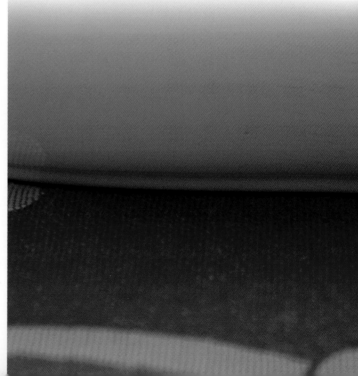

Daging Abon-abon ✺

(Shredded Spicy Beef)

Ingredients

Boneless beef chuck or any stewing cut	450 g (1 lb)
Garlic	2 cloves, peeled and chopped
Brown sugar	1 tsp
Galangal (*laos*)	1 tsp, ground
Coriander (*ketumbar*)	½ tsp, ground
Tamarind (*asam Jawa*) juice (see pg 16)	1 Tbsp
Salt	1 tsp
Vegetable oil	2 Tbsp
Onion	1, small, peeled and thinly sliced

Method

- On the day before, cook meat in water with a bit of salt added until tender. Store cooled, cooked meat in the refrigerator overnight.
- On cooking day, shred cooked beef into small strips, pulling it apart with your fingers.
- Mix together garlic, brown sugar, galangal, coriander, tamarind juice and salt. Add mixture to meat and stir well.
- Heat oil in a heavy frying pan (skillet) and cook meat-cum-spices until deep brown and crisp. Dish out.
- In a clean pan, fry onion slices until deep brown. Sprinkle on top of meat and serve.

Empal Daging ✺

(Diced Spicy Beef)

Ingredients

Beef for stewing	450 g (1 lb)
Salt	1½ tsp
Water	500 ml (2 cups)
Galangal (*laos*)	1 tsp, ground
Tamarind (*asam Jawa*) juice (see pg 16)	1 Tbsp
Vegetable oil	3 Tbsp

Method

- Dice beef into bite-size pieces and cook with salt and water until tender. Allow to cool in bouillon, then drain and remove.
- Drain and remove cooled beef pieces, then rub with galangal and tamarind juice.
- Heat oil in a frying pan (skillet) and fry beef until medium brown. Serve.

Sambal Goreng Daging

(Peppered Beef)

Ingredients

Beef round steak or any tender cut	450 g (1 lb)
Vegetable oil	2 Tbsp
Onion	1, medium, peeled and finely chopped
Garlic	2 cloves, peeled and finely chopped
Galangal (*laos*)	1 tsp, ground
Salt	1 tsp
Dried prawn (shrimp) paste (*terasi*)	1 pea-size piece
Brown sugar	½ tsp
Red chillies	2, thinly sliced
Kaffir lime leaves (*daun jeruk purut*)	2
Salam leaves (*daun salam*)	2
Tamarind (*asam Jawa*) juice (see pg 16)	1 Tbsp
Water or coconut milk (optional)	

Method

- Slice beef thinly and set aside.
- Heat oil in a frying pan (skillet) and lightly sauté onion and garlic.
- Add galangal, salt, dried prawn paste and brown sugar. Fry for several minutes, then add beef slices and mix with spices.
- Add chillies and mix well, then add lime and *salam* leaves and tamarind juice. Fry until deep brown. A little water or coconut milk may be added to prevent drying out and burning. Serve warm.

NOTE: Sambal Goreng Daging, which is common fare the length and breadth of the archipelago, may be made with liver.

Daging Smor

(Braised Beef)

Ingredients

Beef boneless chuck or any stewing cut	450 g (1 lb)
Cooking oil	2 Tbsp
Onions	2, medium, peeled and sliced into thin strips
Nutmeg (*pala*)	½ tsp, ground
Sweet soy sauce (*kecap manis*)	2 Tbsp
Salt	1½ tsp
Water	500 ml (2 cups)

Method

- Cut beef into broad slices. Set aside.
- Heat oil in a frying pan (skillet). Add onions and fry until light brown, then remove and set aside.
- In the same pan, fry beef until golden brown. Add nutmeg and soy sauce. Stir briskly, then add fried onions, salt and water. Cover and simmer until meat is tender. Serve.

Sambal Goreng Hati

(Spicy Beef Liver)

Ingredients

Beef liver	450 g (1 lb)
Salt	a pinch
Onion	1, large, peeled and chopped
Garlic	3 cloves, peeled and chopped
Red chillies	1 or more to taste, crushed
Galangal (*laos*)	1 tsp, ground
Lemon grass (*serai*)	½ tsp, ground
Brown sugar	a pinch
Candlenuts (*kemiri*)	2, grated
Kaffir lime leaves (*daun jeruk purut*)	3
Dried prawn (shrimp) paste (*terasi*)	1 pea-size piece
Tamarind (*asam Jawa*) juice (see pg 16)	1 Tbsp
Salt	1 tsp
Vegetable oil	2 Tbsp
Coconut milk	250 ml (1 cup), squeezed from ½ grated coconut with sufficient water added

Method

- Boil liver in water with a pinch of salt added for about 15 minutes. Drain and remove from stock. Slice and set aside.
- Except oil and coconut milk, combine all remaining ingredients. Sauté mixture in oil for about 2 minutes.
- Add liver and sauté for 2 minutes more. Then, add coconut milk, cover and simmer until almost dry. Serve.

NOTE: Chicken liver may be used as a substitute, but omit boiling it.

Begedel Pedes

(Spicy Beef Croquettes)

Ingredients

Potato	1, medium, peeled
Minced (ground) beef	225 g (7½ oz)
Egg	1, yolk and white separated
Ground black pepper	1 tsp
Nutmeg (*pala*)	a pinch, ground
Salt	½ tsp
Onion	1, medium, peeled and chopped
Breadcrumbs	
Vegetable oil	3 Tbsp

Method

- Boil potato until cooked, then drain and mash.
- Add beef to mashed potato and mix well, then knead in egg yolk. Add pepper, nutmeg and salt, mixing thoroughly. Mix in onion last and shape mixture into patties.
- Beat egg white until foamy and coat patties. Dip coated patties into breadcrumbs and sauté in oil on both sides until brown. Serve.

Opposite: Begedel Pedes

Rempah-rempah ～
(Spicy Meat Cakes)

Ingredients

Minced (ground) beef	225 g (7½ oz)
Onion	1, medium, peeled and finely chopped
Garlic	1 clove, peeled and finely chopped
Coconut	½ cup, desiccated or freshly grated
Dried prawn (shrimp) paste (*terasi*)	1 pea-size piece
Ground black pepper	½ tsp
Coriander (*ketumbar*)	½ tsp, ground
Brown sugar	a pinch
Salt	½ tsp
Egg	1
Vegetable oil for deep-frying	

Method

- Knead beef with onion and garlic in a bowl. Then, thoroughly mix with coconut, dried prawn paste, pepper, coriander, brown sugar and salt. Add egg and mix well.
- Shape mixture into tiny meatballs and deep-fry until medium brown. Drain on absorbent paper towels and serve.

Sapi Kari Palembang ～
(Palembang Curried Beef)

Ingredients

Vegetable oil	2 Tbsp
Onion	1, medium, peeled and sliced
Garlic	2 cloves, peeled and chopped
Red chillies	2 or more to taste, crushed
Cloves (*cengkeh*)	a pinch, ground
Cumin (*jintan*)	a pinch, ground
Ginger	a pinch, ground
Turmeric (*kunyit*)	1 tsp, ground
Beef for stewing	450 g (1 lb), diced
Salt	1½ tsp
Coconut milk	500 ml (2 cups), squeezed from 1 grated coconut with sufficient water added
Salam leaf (*daun salam*)	1
Potato	1, large, peeled, boiled and diced

Method

- Heat oil in a frying pan (skillet). Sauté onion, garlic, chillies, cloves, cumin, ginger and turmeric, taking care not to burn mixture.
- Add beef to spices together with salt. Sauté until spices are absorbed by beef, stirring frequently.
- Add coconut milk and *salam* leaf. Cover and simmer until almost tender.
- Add potato and simmer for about 20 minutes more. Serve warm and garnished with onion strips, if desired.

Opposite: Sapi Kari Palembang

Babi Tulang Cin ❧

(Borneo Spare Ribs)

Ingredients

Pork spare ribs	900 g (2 lb), use meaty ones
Peanut oil	2 Tbsp
Garlic	3 cloves, peeled and finely chopped
Nutmeg (*pala*)	½ tsp, ground
Cloves (*cengkeh*)	a pinch, ground
Ground black pepper	½ tsp
Salt	2 tsp
Brown sugar	1 tsp
Light soy sauce (*kecap asin*)	1 Tbsp
Water	125 ml (½ cup)

Method

- Chop spare ribs into desired serving portions. Set aside.
- Heat oil in a frying pan (skillet). Fry garlic, then add spare ribs to pan and mix thoroughly.
- Add nutmeg, cloves, pepper and salt. Sauté until mixture turns a medium brown.
- Add brown sugar, soy sauce and water. Cover tightly and simmer until tender.

Babi Cin ❧

(Sino-Indonesian Pork)

Ingredients

Potatoes	2, small
Peanut oil	2 Tbsp
Onion	1, medium, peeled and thinly sliced
Garlic	3 cloves, peeled and thinly sliced
Coriander (*ketumbar*)	1 tsp, ground
Cumin (*jintan*)	a pinch, ground
Ground black pepper	½ tsp
Brown sugar	½ tsp
Light soy sauce (*kecap asin*)	1 Tbsp
Salt	1 tsp
Boneless lean pork	450 g (1 lb)
Water	375 ml (1½ cups)

Method

- Boil potatoes in their jackets until cooked. When cool, peel and slice thinly. Set aside.
- Heat oil in a frying pan (skillet) and sauté onion, garlic, coriander, cumin and pepper until light brown.
- Add brown sugar, soy sauce and salt. Combine pork with mixture and fry over low heat for about 10 minutes, stirring frequently.
- Add water, cover and simmer until tender. Then, add sliced potatoes to cooked pork. Serve.

Opposite: Babi Tulang Cin

Babi Bali ✌

(Balinese Pork)

Ingredients

Onion	1, medium, peeled and finely chopped
Garlic	3 cloves, peeled and finely chopped
Peanut oil	1 Tbsp
Red chilli	1 or more to taste, cut or crushed
Coriander (*ketumbar*)	1 tsp, ground
Turmeric (*kunyit*)	1 tsp, ground
Lean pork	450 g (1 lb)
Coconut milk	250 ml (1 cup), squeezed from 1 grated coconut with sufficient water added
Salt	1 tsp

Method

* Sauté onion and garlic in oil together with chilli, coriander and turmeric for about 2 minutes.
* Add pork and sauté for 5 minutes more. Then, add coconut milk and salt. Cover and simmer over low heat until pork is tender. Serve.

NOTE: For a less spicy dish, add in red chilli whole or slit open and discard seeds. If fresh red chillies are unavailable, use dried ones; these have to be soaked in water to soften and drained before use.

Lelawar Babi ✌

(Shredded Spicy Pork)

Ingredients

Boneless pork	450 g (1 lb)
Onion	1, small, peeled and finely chopped
Garlic	2 cloves, peeled and finely chopped
Cumin (*jintan*)	½ tsp, ground
Coriander (*ketumbar*)	1 tsp, ground
Galangal (*laos*)	1 tsp, ground
Salt	1 tsp
Vegetable oil	1 Tbsp
Red chilli	1, sliced either diagonally or into strips
Salam leaf (*daun salam*)	1
Coconut milk	250 ml (1 cup), squeezed from ½ grated coconut with sufficient water added
Tamarind (*asam Jawa*) juice (see pg 16)	1 Tbsp

Method

* Cut pork into thin strips. Mix onion and garlic with pork. Then, rub pork with cumin, coriander, galangal and salt. Set aside.
* Heat oil in a frying pan (skillet) and add pork. Sauté for several minutes.
* Add chilli, *salam* leaf and coconut milk. Simmer, uncovered, until meat is very tender. Then, add tamarind juice. Serve.

NOTE: *Lelawar* is a Balinese style of cooking which explains why pork is used. Beef may be substituted.

Opposite: Lelawar Babi

Babi Masak Kecap ⤳

(Pork in Soy Sauce)

Ingredients

Boneless lean pork	450 g (1 lb), diced
Peanut oil	1 Tbsp
Onions	2, small, peeled and finely chopped
Garlic	3 cloves, peeled and finely chopped
Ginger	a pinch, ground
Brown sugar	1 tsp
Sweet soy sauce (*kecap manis*)	3 Tbsp
Water	125 ml (½ cup)
Salt	1 tsp

Method

- Fry pork in peanut oil until light brown. Add onions and garlic. Stirring constantly, fry until onions turn brown.
- Add all remaining ingredients, cover tightly and simmer 15–20 minutes. Serve.

Babi Berguling ⤳

(Spit-roasted Pig, Bali Style)

Ingredients

Suckling pig	1, about 4.5 kg (10 lb)
Onion	1, large, peeled and finely chopped
Garlic	2 cloves, peeled and finely chopped
Cloves (*cengkeh*)	3 whole
Ginger	1 tsp, ground
Coriander (*ketumbar*)	1 tsp, ground
Red chilli	½, crushed
Salam leaves (*daun salam*)	2
Turmeric (*kunyit*)	4 tsp, ground
Salt	3 Tbsp
Coconut milk	250 ml (1 cup), squeezed from 1 grated coconut with sufficient water added
Coconut	2 Tbsp, desiccated or freshly grated

Method

- Wash pig thoroughly in cool water in preparation for stuffing. Set aside.
- Mix together onion, garlic, cloves, ginger, coriander, chilli and *salam* leaves. Then, add 2 tsp turmeric and 1½ Tbsp salt.
- Stuff pig with above mixture, rubbing interior thoroughly. Sew up cavity.
- Separately mix together remaining turmeric and salt and rub onto pig's skin.
- Skewer pig and roast over red-hot, smokeless charcoal fire. Rotate constantly. Brush pig occasionally with coconut milk mixed with desiccated or freshly grated coconut. Cook for approximately 4 hours until meat is tender and skin crisp.

Bebotok Sapi ∽

(Indonesian Meat Loaf)

Ingredients

Minced (ground) beef	225 g (7½ oz)
Onion	1, small, finely chopped
Garlic	2 cloves, peeled and finely chopped
Candlenuts (*kemiri*)	2, grated
Coriander (*ketumbar*)	1 tsp, ground
Cumin (*jintan*)	a pinch, ground
Ginger	a pinch, ground
Red chillies	½ or more to taste, crushed
Lemon grass (*serai*)	a pinch, ground
Tamarind (*asam Jawa*) juice (see pg 16)	1 Tbsp
Salt	½ tsp
Vegetable oil	2 Tbsp
Coconut milk	250 ml (1 cup), squeezed from ½ grated coconuts with sufficient water added
Egg	1, hard-boiled, shelled and sliced
Aluminium foil	

Method

- Combine beef with onion and garlic. Add candlenuts, then coriander, cumin, ginger, chillies, lemon grass, tamarind juice and salt. Mix well and set aside.

- Heat oil in a frying pan (skillet). Add seasoned beef and fry until medium brown. Pour in coconut milk and simmer until almost dry. Remove from heat.

- Cut aluminium foil into 18-cm (7-inch) squares. Onto each square, place an egg slice and cover with 1 rounded (heaped) Tbsp cooked beef mixture. Wrap meat in foil and seal ends.

- Steam foil parcels in a double-boiler or steamer for about 1 hour. Serve.

NOTE: For variation, use either prawns (shrimps), veal, chicken or fish (cod is excellent) instead of beef. In Indonesia, *bebotok* is wrapped in banana leaves. If you prefer a natural material and banana leaves are unavailable, use cabbage leaves instead of foil. The result is a form of Indonesian stuffed cabbage.

Left: Bebotok Sapi

Braised Pork Roast in Banana Leaves ～

Ingredients

Pork roast	1.15 kg (2 lb 8 oz), butterfly cut
Sea salt	to taste
Ground black pepper	to taste
Spring onions (scallions)	3, chopped
Vegetable oil	1 Tbsp
Banana leaves	2, large, each 60 x 30 cm (24 x 12 inches)

Seasoning

Coriander (*ketumbar*)	¼ tsp, ground
Galangal (*laos*)	¼ tsp, ground
Cloves (*cengkeh*)	2, finely ground
Garlic	1 clove, peeled and finely chopped

Braising liquid

Garlic	5 cloves, peeled and chopped
Galangal (*laos*)	½ tsp, ground
Lesser galangal (*kencur*)	¼ tsp, ground
Light soy sauce (*kecap asin*)	250 ml (1 cup)
Cinnamon (*kayu manis*)	1 stick, 7.5-cm (3-inch) long
Water	125 ml (½ cup)

Method

- Clean and dry roast. Rub with salt, pepper, combined seasoning ingredients and spring onions. Roll up roast and tie with clean string.
- In a heavy Dutch oven, heat oil and brown roast on all sides, about 3 minutes each side. Remove when done and wrap roast loosely with banana leaves.
- Add braising liquid ingredients to Dutch oven and bring to a simmer.
- Lower in banana-leaf wrapped roast and cover tightly. Reduce heat to lowest possible and braise for 2 hours 30 minutes.

NOTE: It is important to use a nice pork roast with some top fat and not tenderloin, which tends to become too dry.

Sambal Goreng Babi ～

(Spicy Pork)

Ingredients

Boneless lean pork	450 g (1 lb), diced
Peanut oil	1 Tbsp
Onion	1, medium, peeled and chopped
Garlic	2 cloves, peeled and chopped
Ginger	a pinch, ground
Red chilli	1 or more to taste, crushed
Sweet soy sauce (*kecap manis*)	1 tsp
Salt	1 tsp
Water	250 ml (1 cup)
Spring onions (scallions)	2, both bulb and shoot, chopped

Method

- Fry pork in peanut oil until light brown.
- Add chopped onion and garlic, stirring frequently until onion is light brown.
- Add ginger, chilli and soy sauce. Mix thoroughly, then add salt and water. Cover and simmer for about 20 minutes.
- Add spring onions and cook over low heat for about 3 minutes. Serve.

Opposite: Sambal Goreng Babi

Satay

Until suburban living burst on the post-war American scene, it was reasonably accurate to observe that the cooking of skewered, diced meat over fiery coals was largely the imprint of Islamic influence on the world's cooking. In a broad scimitar-shaped area, extending from West Africa to Indonesia, skewered meat is one of the lively culinary arts. In Marrakesh and Casablanca, in Beirut and Damascus, Karachi and Dhaka, Ipoh and Singapore, and along the island-chain of Indonesia, roasting bits of meat over a charcoal brazier is deeply embedded in the culture. Moving east of Suez, the marinating and basting sauces for this form of cookery becomes increasingly aromatic, pungent and searing in direct ratio to the abundance and variety of available herbs and spices. The artistic apogee in the preparation of skewered meats is in Indonesia, in the very Spice Islands themselves.

Every country in the Islamic belt lays claim to having originated the art of skewering. Indeed, there are as many claimants as names for this particular style of cooking. The Turks call it *shish-kebab* — *shish* meaning skewer, *kebab* meaning meat. In the Caucasian mountains, along the southern perimeter of Russia, where Islamic influence spread centuries ago, following the trail of spice-laden caravans, it is called *shashlik*. On the Indian subcontinent, the term is romanised as *kebab*. In Southeast Asia, among the Malays and Indonesians, skewering is known as *satay* or *saté*.

The Chinese scoff at the theory that *satay* is Islamic in origin, although it is likely that it entered China through the backdoor, Xinjiang (Sinkiang). The Chinese not only claim to having originated the art, but also contend that the words *satay* and *saté* are Chinese derivatives. According to their version, early migrants from fabled Cathay, pre-dating the arrival of Arab traders and the advent of Islam, filtered southward into the region now called Southeast Asia. They brought with them the custom of roasting or grilling bits of pork, pierced on bamboo sticks, over red-hot charcoals. Invariably, for convenience as much as habit, the Chinese slipped three pieces of meat — never more, never less — onto the bamboo skewer. *Satay*, say the Chinese, therefore comes from the south Chinese words *sah* (three) and *tay* (piece).

Gradually, the Malays and Indonesians copied the technique and, conceded the Chinese, crowned it with the decisive embellishment: spicy marination and a unique peanut sauce. With the adoption of Islam, which proscribes the pig, the Malay peoples substituted lamb, beef, fowl and seafood for pork.

Today, the street hawker's cry of *satay* is as common in Indonesia as the chirp of the cricket in the evening. Barefoot peddlers in sarongs carrying a portable, charcoal stove, patter through coastal ports, inland towns and villages calling out their wares for all to hear. They are the masters of the trade and their *satay* is unrivalled. Often, while my husband covered cabinet sessions in Jakarta that lasted into dawn, we would squat with Indonesian newsmen outside the Premier's office at Pejambon, swapping *kabar angin* (literally, 'news on the wind'), while munching freshly grilled *satay kambing* made from marinated slivers of goat.

Personally, I have always found pork, chicken, lamb and goat the most succulent meats for *satay*. Quite unabashedly, I have always been glad that Muslims may not eat pork — that leaves that much more for the rest of us! However, on the Hindu island of Bali and among the Christian enclaves on Ambon, Maluku, in Sulawesi and Sumatra, pork *satay* is, unfortunately, a prized dish. No festive occasion is complete without a touch of pork.

In contemporary America, with the emphasis on outdoor living and cooking, *satay*, *saté*, *shashlik*, *kebab*, skewered meat — call it what you will — has made a deep and probably lasting inroad into eating habits. Tragically, skewering in America is often the victim of the 'bigger and better' philosophy. The pieces of meat used are invariably far too large, the cooking coals aflame instead of inwardly afire and skewers are sometimes laden like garbage scows with pineapples, tomatoes, etc., all at the expense of the meat. Harsh judgement? Perhaps. Though it makes the unskillful laugh, it cannot but make the artist grieve.

To skewer *satay* skillfully and successfully in the Indonesian fashion, six factors should be constantly borne in mind: (1) the charcoal, (2) the skewer, (3) the size and quality of the cuts, (4) rotation, (5) the preparation of the marinating and basting mixtures and (6) the preparation of the peanut sauce.

In order, then: first, the charcoals. What applies here applies to all outdoor cooking. In the impatient West, barbecues are often hastily prepared. The cook lights the charcoal (eventually), fans the air briskly and while the flames leap higher, starts to grill the meat. The end result, euphonically termed "charcoal broiled", is often so burnt and blackened beyond recognition as to cause courteous guests to adopt a grin-and-bear-it posture. A cardinal rule in outdoor cooking is to fan the burning charcoals until the coals glow evenly without the presence of a flame. Think of the Indian fakir and his bed of live coals the next time you barbecue.

Next, the skewer. It should be as slender as the proverbial reed and tapered towards the tip like a fly-rod. Bamboo sticks, inexpensive and easily obtainable in Japanese gift and food shops in the West, are ideal and may be used repeatedly if you wrap the holding ends in aluminium foil before thrusting onto the red-hot coals. Metal skewers are as good but avoid those with rapier points. In *satay*, the meat is not removed from the skewer before eating but is eaten straight from the stick. Too sharp a metal object is dangerous. Since *satay* is eaten from the skewer, the size of the portions should be relatively small, only slightly larger than a radish. This not only makes the meat easier to pull from the skewer, but facilitates the marination. Tender meat is advisable; top quality meat is recommended. Commercial tenderiser is useful; in Indonesia (as in Surinam), the wrapping of meat in papaya leaves does the tenderising trick. In the preparation of chicken *satay*, use only the breast.

During the skewering, keep an eye on the meat, rotating from time to time to ensure even cooking and no burning. In the preparation of *satay*, the marinating sauce, used also for the basting process, is a key to ultimate success. Similarly, the *saus kacang* or peanut sauce, without which *satay* is like rolls without butter, must be carefully prepared.

Indonesian *satay* accompanied by peanut sauce is an incomparable outdoor dish. Learn the knack of making it and you will be serving it often through the summer season. It is delightful with a glass of beer. With rice and just one Indonesian-styled vegetable, *satay* constitutes a meal worthy of praise. Served as a snack, *satay* is an ideal cocktail titbit. A word of caution, however: there is never enough to go around.

Satay Ayam ⟿

(Chicken Satay)

Ingredients

Chicken breasts	2, each 360 g (12 oz)
Bamboo or metal skewers	
Vegetable oil	3 Tbsp
Sweet soy sauce (*kecap manis*)	2 Tbsp
Tamarind (*asam Jawa*) juice (see pg 16)	1 Tbsp
Coriander (*ketumbar*)	½ tsp

Method

- Skin chicken breasts, if desired, and cut into bite-size portions. Thread onto bamboo or metal skewers. Set aside.
- Heat oil in a saucepan. Add all remaining ingredients. Heat through before removing from heat.
- Using a soft-tufted cake brush, paint chicken thoroughly with cooked sauce.
- Place prepared sticks in a circular fashion over red-hot charcoals. Rotate skewers often and baste frequently to prevent chicken from drying out. Serve immediately when done.

Satay Ayam Kuning ⟿

(Yellow Chicken Satay)

Ingredients

Chicken breasts	2, each 360 g (12 oz)
Bamboo or metal skewers	
Vegetable oil	3 Tbsp
Coriander (*ketumbar*)	½ tsp
Cumin (*jintan*)	a pinch, ground
Turmeric (*kunyit*)	1 tsp, ground
Salt	½ tsp
Tamarind (*asam Jawa*) juice (see pg 16)	1 Tbsp

Method

- Skin chicken breasts, if desired, and cut into bite-size portions. Thread onto bamboo or meat skewers. Set aside.
- Heat oil in saucepan. Add coriander, cumin, turmeric, salt and tamarind juice. Heat through before removing from heat.
- Using a soft-tufted cake brush, paint chicken thoroughly with spice mixture.
- Cook meat over charcoal heat until well done.

Satay Babi ⚬

(Pork Satay)

Ingredients

Boneless lean pork	450 g (1 lb)
Garlic	1 clove, peeled
Candlenuts (*kemiri*)	2, grated
Dried prawn (shrimp) paste (*terasi*)	1 tsp, softened in 2 Tbsp water
Dark soy sauce	2 Tbsp
Peanut oil	2 Tbsp
Bamboo or metal skewers	

Method

- Cut pork into thin slices. Set aside.
- Mix together garlic, candlenuts, dried prawn paste, soy sauce and peanut oil.
- Add pork to seasoning mixture and leave for 2 hours, permitting meat to soak up seasoning.
- Thread pork onto skewers and broil (grill) over charcoal. Serve.

NOTE: Pork requires slightly more cooking time than chicken or beef.

Satay Babi Kuning ⚬

(Yellow Pork Satay)

Ingredients

Boneless lean pork	450 g (1 lb)
Onion	1, small, peeled and finely chopped
Garlic	1 clove, peeled and finely chopped
Candlenut (*kemiri*)	1, grated
Galangal (*laos*)	½ tsp, ground
Coriander (*ketumbar*)	½ tsp, ground
Turmeric (*kunyit*)	1 tsp, ground
Coconut milk	125 ml (½ cup), squeezed from ½ grated coconut with sufficient water added
Vegetable oil	1 Tbsp
Salt	1 tsp
Bamboo or metal skewers	

Method

- Cut pork into thin slices. Set aside.
- Except pork, mix together all remaining ingredients. Then, mix in pork and leave to marinate for at least 2 hours.
- Thread marinated pork onto skewers and broil (grill) over charcoal. Serve.

Satay Kambing ✤

(Mutton Satay)

Ingredients

Boneless mutton	450 g (1 lb)
Onion	1, small, peeled
Garlic	2 cloves, peeled
Vegetable oil	2 Tbsp
Dried prawn (shrimp) paste (*terasi*)	1 tsp, softened in 2 Tbsp water
Dark soy sauce	1 Tbsp
Brown sugar	1 tsp

Method

- Cut mutton into bite-size portions and set aside.
- Chop onion and garlic together.
- Put all ingredients into a bowl and mix well. Leave for at least 2 hours.
- Thread seasoned meat onto skewers and broil (grill) over charcoal. Serve.

Satay Ayam Madura ✤

(Madura Chicken Satay)

Ingredients

Chicken breasts	2, each 360 g (12 oz)
Vegetable oil	3 Tbsp
Onion	1, small, peeled and finely chopped
Garlic	1 clove, peeled and finely chopped
Candlenuts (*kemiri*)	2, grated
Coconut	2 Tbsp, desiccated or freshly grated
Coriander (*ketumbar*)	1 tsp
Sambal oelek (see pg 159)	1 tsp
Lemon grass (*serai*)	½ tsp, ground
Dried prawn (shrimp) paste (*terasi*)	1 pea-size piece, softened in 2 Tbsp water
Brown sugar	1 tsp
Bamboo or metal skewers	

Method

- Skin chicken breasts, if desired, and cut into bite-size cubes and set aside.
- Heat oil in a saucepan and add all remaining ingredients. Stir well and heat through before removing from heat.
- Add chicken cubes to cooked mixture and leave for at least 1 hour to allow aromatic and pungent spices to be absorbed.
- Skewer marinated meat and cook until well done over charcoal heat. Serve.

Opposite: Satay Ayam Madura

Satay Udang ❧

(Prawn Satay)

Ingredients

Prawns (shrimps)	450 g (1 lb), approximately 24, peeled and cleaned
Garlic	2 cloves, peeled and minced
Light soy sauce (*kecap asin*)	1 Tbsp
Sweet soy sauce (*kecap manis*)	1 Tbsp
Fresh ginger	1 tsp, minced
Coriander (*ketumbar*)	¼ tsp, ground
Cooking oil	1 Tbsp
Bamboo skewers	

Method

- Season prawns with garlic, both soy sauces, ginger and coriander. Leave to marinate for at least 1 hour in the refrigerator.
- Thread 3 seasoned prawns onto each skewer.
- Cook prepared prawn *satay* over charcoal heat until pink. If cooking indoors, cook prawns under broiler (grill) but cover the tips of skewers with aluminium foil to prevent burning. Alternatively, soak bamboo skewers in water before use.

Satay Udang sama Hati ❧

(Prawn and Liver Satay)

Ingredients

Fresh prawns (shrimps)	450 g (1 lb)
Beef liver	225 g (7½ oz)
Water	250 ml (1 cup)
Bamboo or metal skewers	
Butter or margarine	2 Tbsp
Garlic	1 clove, peeled and chopped
Dark soy sauce	1 Tbsp
Tamarind (*asam Jawa*) juice (see pg 16)	1 Tbsp
Salt	1 tsp

Method

- Boil prawns in sufficient water for 15 minutes, then peel and devein. Set aside.
- Boil liver in 250 ml (1 cup) water for about 15 minutes. Drain and cut cooked liver into small pieces.
- Skewer prawn and liver in alternating fashion; first prawn, then liver, then prawn and so on. Set aside.
- Melt butter or margarine in saucepan and add all remaining ingredients. Brush skewered prawns and liver thoroughly with cooked mixture.
- Broil (grill) quickly over red-hot coals and serve.

Opposite: Satay Udang sama Hati

Satay Sapi Pedes ~
(Hot Beef Satay)

Ingredients

Boneless beef sirloin	450 g (1 lb)
Onion	1, small, peeled and finely chopped
Vegetable oil	3 Tbsp
Sambal oelek (see pg 159)	1 tsp
Candlenuts (*kemiri*)	2, grated
Coriander (*ketumbar*)	1 tsp, ground
Ginger	a pinch, ground
Tamarind (*asam Jawa*) juice (see pg 16)	2 Tbsp

Method

- Cut meat into bite-size portions. Set aside.
- In a saucepan, sauté onion in oil until medium brown. Remove from heat and set aside.
- Mix together all remaining ingredients. Add resulting mixture to sautéed onions, then mix in beef and leave for 15 minutes.
- Thread seasoned meat onto skewers and broil (grill) quickly over charcoal heat. Serve.

Satay Sapi ~
(Beef Satay)

Ingredients

Boneless beef sirloin or any tender cut	450 g (1 lb)
Vegetable oil	2 Tbsp
Sweet soy sauce (*kecap manis*)	1 Tbsp
Tamarind (*asam Jawa*) juice (see pg 16)	1 Tbsp

Method

- Cut beef into bite-size portions. Set aside.
- Heat oil in a small saucepan, then mix in soy sauce and tamarind juice. Heat through and remove.
- Add beef to cooked sauce and leave for 15 minutes, then thread onto skewers.
- Broil (grill) over charcoal heat until done. Serve.

Opposite: Satay Sapi Pedes

Satay Sapi Manis ∽
(Sweet Beef Satay)

Ingredients

Boneless beef sirloin	450 g (1 lb)
Vegetable oil	2 Tbsp
Brown sugar	1 tsp
Sweet soy sauce (*kecap manis*)	2 Tbsp
Salt	½ tsp

Method

- Cut meat into bite-size portions. Set aside.
- Heat oil in a saucepan and add brown sugar, soy sauce and salt. Heat through and remove from heat.
- Add meat to cooked sauce and leave for 15 minutes, then thread onto skewers.
- Broil (grill) quickly over charcoal heat. Serve.

Satay Tusuk Anak Sapi ∽
(Veal Satay)

Ingredients

Boneless veal	450 g (1 lb)
Onion	1, small, peeled and finely chopped
Vegetable oil	1 Tbsp
Turmeric (*kunyit*)	½ tsp, ground
Lemon grass (*serai*)	a pinch, ground
Coriander (*ketumbar*)	1 tsp, ground
Salt	1 tsp
Brown sugar	1 tsp
Dried prawn (shrimp) paste (*terasi*)	1 pea-size piece
Tamarind (*asam Jawa*) juice (see pg 16)	1 Tbsp
Coconut milk	250 ml (1 cup), squeezed from ½ grated coconut with sufficient water added
Bamboo or metal skewers	

Method

- Cut veal into bite-size portions. Set aside.
- In a saucepan, sauté onion lightly in oil. Then, add turmeric, lemon grass and coriander. Stir and sauté again.
- Add meat to pan with salt and brown sugar. Sauté lightly.
- Add all remaining ingredients, cover saucepan and cook until almost dry.
- Remove meat and thread onto skewers.
- Hold skewers over red-hot coals for only a few minutes and serve immediately.

Saus Kacang Pedes ✥

(Hot Peanut Sauce)

Ingredients

Onion	1, medium, peeled and finely sliced
Garlic	1 clove, peeled and finely sliced
Vegetable oil or margarine	1 Tbsp
Creamy peanut butter	3 Tbsp
Water	125 ml (½ cup)
Sambal oelek (see pg 159)	2 tsp
Brown sugar	1 tsp
Sweet soy sauce (kecap manis)	1 Tbsp
Tamarind (asam Jawa) juice (see pg 16)	1 Tbsp
Dried prawn (shrimp) paste (terasi)	1 pea-size piece
Salt	½ tsp

Method

- Sauté onion and garlic in oil or margarine until deep brown. Remove from pan and drain on absorbent paper towels.
- Add peanut butter and water to saucepan and bring to the boil. Turn off heat and stir until the consistency of paste is achieved.
- Add in sambal oelek, sugar, soy sauce, tamarind juice, dried prawn paste and salt. Mix well.
- Lastly, add onion and garlic and stir gently. Serve lukewarm or cool.

NOTE: For variation, omit onion.

Sambal Kecap ✥

(Spicy Soy Sauce)

Ingredients

Dark soy sauce	4 Tbsp
Red chilli	1, sliced
Tamarind (asam Jawa) juice (see pg 16)	1 tsp
Crisp-fried onion slices	1 Tbsp

Method

- Mix all ingredients together and serve with satay.

Saus Kacang Tidak Pedes ⁊

(Bland Peanut Sauce)

Ingredients

Creamy peanut butter	4 Tbsp
Water	180 ml (¾ cup)
Garlic	1 clove, peeled and finely chopped
Dried prawn (shrimp) paste (*terasi*)	1 pea-size piece
Brown sugar	1 tsp
Dark soy sauce	1 Tbsp
Tamarind (*asam Jawa*) juice (see pg 16)	1 Tbsp
Salt	1 tsp

Method

- Mix peanut butter and water in a saucepan and bring to the boil. Turn off heat and stir until the consistency of paste is achieved.
- Add all remaining ingredients and stir well. Serve lukewarm with *satay*.

Saus Kacang Baru ⁊

(Fresh Peanut Sauce)

Ingredients

Onion	1, small, peeled and thinly sliced
Garlic	2 cloves, peeled and thinly sliced
Peanut oil	1 Tbsp
Peanuts	1 cup, shelled and roasted
Lemon grass (*serai*)	1 stalk
Lesser galangal (*kencur*)	1 piece, peeled
Dried prawn (shrimp) paste (*terasi*)	1 Tbsp
Red chilli	1, crushed
Brown sugar	1 tsp
Dark soy sauce	1 Tbsp
Salt	½ tsp
Tamarind (*asam Jawa*) juice (see pg 16)	2 Tbsp

Method

- Fry onion and garlic in oil until brown.
- Put fried onion and garlic, peanuts, lemon grass, lesser galangal and dried prawn paste into a blender (processor); blend until fine. Transfer to a bowl.
- To blended mixture, add all remaining ingredients. Mix together thoroughly, then add sufficient boiling water to make a thick paste.
- Serve with *satay*.

Opposite: Sauce Kacang Baru

Vegetables

Vegetables on the Spice Islands are familiar to Westerners; indeed, some are of New World origin. With scattered exceptions, an Indonesian buying vegetables in a European or American market would feel completely at home — glass, chromium, stainless steel and fluorescent lights notwithstanding.

Climate, of course, is the factor controlling the cultivation of all plant life, including vegetables, and climate depends largely on altitude. Although the Malay world is situated along the equator, it rises from below sea level to snow-capped peaks. Java, Sumatra and Sulawesi are studded with a jumble of active and extinct volcanoes and escarpments. Rivers rush down the mountain slopes and deposit volcanic silt into valleys and onto lowlands. The result is an enriched soil.

Although Java is crowded to bursting point, with a population upwards of 100 million people, the island still has pockets of rain forests and bamboo groves. At different elevations, the heat and humidity of the island subtly changes, as does the island's produce. From sea level to 305 metres (1,000 feet), rice and rubber flourish; at 1,524 metres (5,000 feet), strawberries; above 1,524 metres (5,000 feet), tea, coffee and orchids, and at extreme altitudes, rhododendrons, maple and a wide variety of 'Western' vegetables. In a real sense, Indonesia is the world's largest greenhouse, shaped like a pyramid and with controlled temperature and humidity at ascending levels.

Curiously, in Indonesia, the temperate and torrid zones share the same latitude. In Irian Jaya (Western New Guinea), the pinnacle is reached, with snow-trimmed mountains. Thus, in Indonesia, it is possible to cultivate a wide variety of completely unrelated vegetables, from bamboo shoots and breadfruit to cauliflower and cabbage. Indonesian cookery has exploited this natural advantage. The result is very often a familiar 'Western' vegetable in a strange setting.

Some Indonesian vegetables, of course, are exotic, such as the flower of the papaya tree. Others are relatively common and reflect a large measure of Chinese cooking influence on the islands: snow peas (young peas in pod) and bean sprouts. For the most part, however, Indonesians use familiar vegetables. Among them are *bayem*, *terung* and *ketimun* (spinach, aubergine/eggplant and cucumber). And there are *kacang*

kaprie and *kacang panjang* (peas and yard-long beans). Other Indonesian favourites have Dutch names, which indicate that they may be European in origin and most probably were introduced during the Dutch colonial century. These include *kol* or *kool* (cabbage), *buncis* (string beans), *wortel* (carrot) and *tomat* (tomato).

Indonesians delight in one vegetable that Europeans do not generally eat but is immensely popular in the Americas, North, Central and South. This is *jagung* or corn. Indeed, on the island of Madura, off the northeastern coast of Java, corn is the staple, not rice. The Madurese roast their corn over hot coals or like most of the islanders, fashion them into small cakes.

Peas are also extremely popular the length and breadth of Indonesia. They are not served as a dish by themselves, however; rather, a handful of peas is scattered into different vegetable dishes, almost at random. In their cooking of vegetables, the Indonesians also make greater use of Chinese flowering cabbage (*sawi*) and leeks (*prei*) more than any other people.

In the vegetable recipes that follow, I have eliminated the picturesque but hard-to-procure vegetables and concentrated on the use of familiar vegetables. Many of these vegetable dishes are ideally suited for a Western buffet.

Two points should be made in advance: the recipes using *sambal oelek* or its substitute, Italian-style crushed red pepper, are fiery and dry. The mild-tasting vegetables are usually not only mild, but also wet. Indeed, Sayur Lodeh, a common vegetable dish in Indonesia, takes the form of a soup, although it is not served as a soup course. You merely pour the vegetables and their broth over your rice and add side-dishes. In some of the following recipes, such as Cap Cai Ca, Chinese influence is manifest.

Some of the Indonesian vegetable dishes call for the use of prawns or shrimps. At first glance, it would appear that these recipes have been misplaced in this volume and belong under the *Fish and Other Seafood* heading, but these dishes are essentially vegetable dishes. To bring out the flavour of certain vegetables, the Indonesians have ingeniously developed the technique of using prawns. I have never found this method employed anywhere else outside of Southeast Asia and nowhere to such an extent as in the archipelago.

Sambal Goreng Buncis

(Peppered String Beans)

Ingredients

String beans	450 g (1 lb)
Onion	1, medium, peeled and thinly sliced
Vegetable oil	1 Tbsp
Red chilli	1, crushed
Lemon grass (*serai*)	1 tsp, ground
Galangal (*laos*)	1 tsp, ground
Brown sugar	½ tsp
Cloves (*cengkeh*)	a pinch, ground
Salt	1 tsp
Dried prawn (shrimp) paste (*terasi*)	1 tsp, softened in 2 Tbsp water
Coconut milk	125 ml (½ cup), squeezed from ½ grated coconut with sufficient water added

Method

- Remove strings from beans and slice each bean into 3 segments. Set aside.
- Sauté onion lightly in oil together with chilli, lemon grass, galangal, brown sugar, cloves and salt.
- Add dried prawn paste and string beans. Sauté about 3 minutes, mixing thoroughly.
- Add coconut milk, cover tightly and cook over low heat until string beans are tender. Serve warm.

Sambal Goreng Hati sama Buncis

(Spicy String Beans with Chicken Liver)

Ingredients

String beans	450 g (1 lb)
Chicken livers	3, thinly sliced
Vegetable oil	1 Tbsp
Onion	1, small, peeled and finely chopped
Turmeric (*kunyit*)	½ tsp, ground
Cloves (*cengkeh*)	a pinch, ground
Lemon grass (*serai*)	½ tsp
Brown sugar	1 tsp
Red chilli	1, crushed
Salt	1 tsp
Coconut milk	60 ml (¼ cup), squeezed from ⅓ grated coconut with sufficient water added
Dried prawn (shrimp) paste (*terasi*)	1 pea-size piece, softened in 2 Tbsp water

Method

- Remove strings from beans and slice each bean in half. Set aside.
- Sauté chicken livers in oil with onion, stirring frequently.
- Add turmeric, cloves, lemon grass, brown sugar, chilli and salt. Sauté for 2 minutes.
- Add string beans followed by coconut milk. Mix thoroughly and add dried prawn paste. Cover and cook over low heat until tender.

NOTE: This dish improves in flavour if left overnight in the refrigerator and then reheated before serving.

Opposite: Sambal Goreng Hati sama Buncis

Sayur Bayem ❧

(Indonesian-style Spinach)

Ingredients

Spinach	450 g (1 lb)
Onion	1, small, peeled and finely sliced
Garlic	1 clove, peeled and chopped
Coconut milk	500 ml (2 cups), squeezed from ½ grated coconut with sufficient water added
Dried prawn (shrimp) paste (*terasi*)	1 pea-size piece
Salt	to taste

Method

- Wash spinach thoroughly and set aside.
- Put onion and garlic in a saucepan with coconut milk, dried prawn paste and salt. Bring to the boil.
- Add spinach and cook, uncovered, until tender. Serve.

Sayur Kool ❧

(Indonesian Cabbage)

Ingredients

Vegetable oil	1 Tbsp
Onion	1, small, peeled and finely chopped
Garlic	1 clove, peeled and finely chopped
Cabbage	1, medium, coarsely cut
Coconut milk	500 ml (2 cups), squeezed from ½ grated coconut with sufficient water added
Dried prawn (shrimp) paste (*terasi*)	1 pea-size piece
Red chilli	1, crushed
Salt	1½ tsp
Fresh or frozen prawns (shrimps)	225 g (7½ oz), peeled
Tamarind (*asam Jawa*) juice (see pg 16)	1 Tbsp

Method

- Heat oil in a frying pan (skillet). Add onion and garlic and fry lightly, then add cabbage and sauté until wilted.
- Pour in coconut milk and add dried prawn paste, chilli and salt. Bring to the boil.
- Add prawns and cook, uncovered, for about 10 minutes, stirring constantly.
- Lastly, add tamarind juice and serve.

Sambal Goreng Kool

(Hot Cabbage Sauté)

Ingredients

Onion	1, medium, peeled and thinly sliced
Vegetable oil	1 Tbsp
Red chilli	1 or more to taste, crushed
Dried prawn (shrimp) paste (*terasi*)	1 pea-size piece
Brown sugar	1 tsp
Galangal (*laos*)	1 tsp, ground
Salt	1 tsp
Cabbage	1, medium, coarsely cut

Method

- Sauté onion lightly in oil. Add chilli, dried prawn paste, brown sugar, galangal and salt. Sauté for about 1 minute, mixing frequently.
- Add cabbage, stir to mix and cover. Cook over low heat until cabbage wilts. If necessary, add a small amount of water or coconut milk to prevent burning. Serve warm.

Sambal Goreng Tempe ⁄∕⁄

(Spicy Fermented Soy Bean Cakes)

Ingredients

Fermented soy bean cakes (*tempe*)	3, thinly sliced
Cooking oil	1 Tbsp and enough for deep-frying
Onion	1, peeled and thinly sliced
Garlic	4 cloves, peeled and chopped
Red chillies	3, thinly sliced
Galangal (*laos*)	1 tsp, ground
Brown sugar	1 tsp
Tamarind (*asam Jawa*) juice (see pg 16)	1 Tbsp
Dried prawns (shrimps)	100 g (½ cup), soaked in water for about 30 minutes and drained before use

Method

- Deep-fry sliced soy bean cakes in hot oil. Drain and set aside.
- In a clean frying pan (skillet), fry onion, garlic and chillies in 1 Tbsp oil. Add galangal, brown sugar and tamarind juice and stir to combine.
- Mix in fried soy bean cakes and pre-soaked prawns. Fry for several minutes more then serve.

NOTE: If you happen to be in a lazy mood, here is a short cut. Fry soy bean cakes, drain and mix with 1 Tbsp ready-made *sambal oelek* or any available prepared *sambal*. Presto — Sambal Goreng Tempe.

Sambal Goreng Terung ⁄∕⁄

(Peppery Aubergines)

Ingredients

Aubergines (eggplants/brinjals)	2, small
Tamarind (*asam Jawa*) juice (see pg 16)	1 Tbsp
Salt	½ tsp
Onion	1, small, thinly sliced
Vegetable oil	2 Tbsp
Coriander (*ketumbar*)	1 tsp, ground
Brown sugar	½ tsp
Red chilli	1 or more to taste, crushed
Dried prawn (shrimp) paste (*terasi*)	1 pea-size piece, softened in 1 Tbsp water

Method

- Peel aubergines and slice thinly. If a firmer texture is preferred, leave skin on and slice. Sprinkle with tamarind juice and salt. Set aside.
- Sauté onion lightly in oil, then add coriander, brown sugar, chilli and dried prawn paste. Stir well.
- Add aubergine slices and mix thoroughly with onion and spices. Cook, uncovered, for about 10 minutes. A little water may be added to prevent burning. Serve warm.

NOTE: Never cover pan, otherwise aubergines will soften to the consistency of a paste.

Opposite: Sambal Goreng Tempe

Sambal Goreng Tomat ～

(Peppered Tomatoes)

Ingredients

Vegetable oil	1 Tbsp
Onion	1, small, peeled and finely sliced
Garlic	1 clove, peeled and finely chopped
Red chilli	1 or more to taste, crushed
Galangal (*laos*)	1 tsp, ground
Salt	½ tsp
Firm tomatoes	4, preferably partially ripe, quartered
Brown sugar	1 tsp
Salt	½ tsp
Coconut milk	60 ml (¼ cup), squeezed from ⅓ grated coconut with sufficient water added

Method

- Heat oil in a frying pan (skillet). Add onion, garlic, chilli, galangal and salt. Sauté lightly.
- Add tomato quarters, brown sugar and salt. Mix thoroughly.
- Add coconut milk, cover and cook tomatoes until the consistency of porridge is achieved. Serve.

Sambal Goreng Bloemkool ～

(Peppered Cauliflower)

Ingredients

Cauliflower	1 head, medium
Vegetable oil	1 Tbsp
Onion	1, small, peeled and thinly sliced
Galangal (*laos*)	1 tsp
Red chilli	1 or more to taste, crushed
Dried prawn (shrimp) paste (*terasi*)	1 pea-size piece
Brown sugar	½ tsp
Salt	1 tsp
Coconut milk	250 ml (1 cup), squeezed from 1 grated coconut with sufficient water added

Method

- Cut cauliflower or pull apart to make florets. Set aside.
- Heat oil in a frying pan (skillet) and sauté onion lightly.
- Add cauliflower florets and sauté 2–3 minutes.
- Add galangal, chilli, dried prawn paste, brown sugar and salt. Sauté 1 minute more.
- Add coconut milk and cover tightly. Reduce heat and cook until florets are tender. Serve.

Opposite: Sambal Goreng Bloemkool

Sambal Goreng Tahu

(Peppered Bean Curd)

Ingredients

Firm bean curd	3 pieces
Vegetable oil	2 Tbsp
Onion	1, small, peeled and chopped
Ginger	a pinch, ground
Garlic	2 cloves, peeled and finely chopped
Spring onion (scallion)	1, finely chopped
Red chilli	1, finely chopped
Celery	1 stalk, finely chopped
Salt	½ tsp
Dark soy sauce	1 Tbsp

Method

- Slice bean curd into thin pieces, then sauté in oil until light brown and remove.
- In the same pan, sauté onion and ginger until light brown. Then, return bean curd to pan and add garlic, spring onion, chilli, celery and salt. Sauté until almost tender.
- Add soy sauce and stir until an even colour is achieved. Serve.

Sayur Asam

(Sour Vegetables)

Ingredients

String beans	450 g (1 lb), strings removed and each cut into thirds
Onion	1, small, peeled and finely chopped
Garlic	1 clove, peeled and finely chopped
Tamarind (*asam Jawa*) juice (see pg 16)	2 Tbsp
Dried prawn (shrimp) paste (*terasi*)	1 pea-size piece
Galangal (*laos*)	1 tsp, ground
Salt	1½ tsp
Fresh or frozen prawns (shrimps)	450 g (1 lb), peeled

Method

- Except prawns, put all other ingredients into a saucepan. Stir, cover and cook over low heat until beans are tender.
- Add prawns and bring to the boil. Then, reduce heat and cook, uncovered, for 10 minutes. Serve.

NOTE: Add a handful of shelled raw peanuts for flavouring.

Begedel Jagung

(Corn Croquettes)

Ingredients

Young corn	3 ears
Spring onion (scallion)	1, finely chopped
Galangal (*laos*)	½ tsp, ground
Coriander (*ketumbar*)	½ tsp, ground
Ground black pepper	a pinch
Plain (all-purpose) flour	2 Tbsp
Eggs	2
Salt	a pinch
Vegetable oil or margarine	3 Tbsp

Method

- Remove kernels from cob, slicing downward in swift strokes with a paring knife.
- Except oil or margarine, mix together all other ingredients, including freshly cut corn, to make a batter. Set aside.
- Heat oil or melt margarine in a frying pan (skillet) and pour in batter by the tablespoon, forming round cakes.
- Fry on both sides until done, then serve. Makes about 8 delicious cakes.

NOTE: The batter may also be deep-fried in a large amount of hot oil.

Opposite: Begedel Jagung

Sambal Goreng Lombok

(Lombok Chilli Sauté)

Ingredients

Green chillies	12
Vegetable oil	2 Tbsp
Onion	1, small, peeled and finely chopped
Garlic	2 cloves, peeled and finely chopped
Brown sugar	1 tsp
Dried prawn (shrimp) paste (*terasi*)	1 pea-size piece
Tamarind (*asam Jawa*) juice (see pg 16)	1 Tbsp
Salt	½ tsp
Coconut milk	60 ml (¼ cup), squeezed from ⅓ grated coconut with sufficient water added

Method

- Cut chillies lengthways, remove seeds and membranes and slice thinly. Set aside.
- Heat oil in a frying pan (skillet). Sauté onion and garlic lightly together with brown sugar, dried prawn paste, tamarind juice and salt.
- Add chillies and sauté until wilted.
- Finally, add coconut milk and cook, uncovered, until almost dry. Serve.

Sayur Lodeh

(Vegetables and Prawns)

Although this common vegetable dish takes the form of a soup, it is not served as a soup course. The vegetables and their broth are poured over the rice and side-dishes are added.

Ingredients

Vegetable oil	1 Tbsp
Onion	1, medium, peeled and thinly sliced
Garlic	1 clove, peeled and finely sliced
Coriander (*ketumbar*)	1 tsp, ground
Galangal (*laos*)	1 tsp, ground
Fresh or frozen prawns (shrimps)	225 g (7½ oz), peeled and cut into thin pieces
Red chilli	1, crushed
Cabbage	225 g (7½ oz), coarsely chopped
Cauliflower	225 g (7½ oz), parted into florets
Carrot	1, small, peeled if desired and diced
String beans	225 g (7½ oz), strings removed and cut into thirds
Aubergine (eggplant/brinjal)	1, small, cubed
Salt	1½ tsp
Coconut milk	750 ml (3 cups), squeezed from 1 grated coconut with sufficient water added
Salam leaf (*daun salam*)	1

Methods

- Heat oil in pan and sauté onion lightly. Add garlic, coriander and galangal. Fry for 1 minute.
- Add prawns and sauté for 2 minutes.
- Add chilli, cabbage, cauliflower, carrot, string beans, aubergine and salt. Cover and cook over low heat for about 10 minutes.
- Pour in coconut milk and add *salam* leaf. Cook, uncovered, stirring almost continuously, until vegetables are tender. Serve.

NOTE: Chicken can be used instead of prawns, chicken breast being preferable.

Opposite: Sayur Lodeh

Sayur Kari ∾

(Curried Vegetables)

Ingredients

Vegetable oil	1 Tbsp
Turmeric (*kunyit*)	1 tsp, ground
Cumin (*jintan*)	½ tsp, ground
Galangal (*laos*)	½ tsp, ground
Coriander (*ketumbar*)	½ tsp, ground
Carrot	1, peeled if desired and cubed
Potatoes	2, medium, peeled and diced
Coconut milk	500 ml (2 cups), squeezed from 1 grated coconut with sufficient water added
Salt	to taste
Aubergine (eggplant/brinjal)	1, small, peeled and diced
String beans	225 g (7½ oz), strings removed strings and cut into thirds
Cabbage	225 g (7½ oz), coarsely chopped

Method

- Heat oil in a frying pan (skillet). Add turmeric, cumin, galangal and coriander. Sauté lightly.
- Add carrot and potatoes with half the coconut milk. Add salt to taste. Cover and cook for about 10 minutes.
- Add all remaining ingredients, cover and continue cooking until carrots and potatoes are tender. Serve.

Sambal Goreng Prei ∾

(Peppered Leeks)

Ingredients

Leeks	450 g (1 lb)
Vegetable oil	1 Tbsp
Red chilli	1 or more to taste, crushed
Brown sugar	½ tsp
Salt	1 tsp
Tamarind (*asam Jawa*) juice (see pg 16)	1 Tbsp
Coconut milk	60 ml (¼ cup), squeezed from ½ grated coconut with sufficient water added

Method

- Wash leeks well to remove all traces of sand and grit. Drain. Slice cleaned leeks into 2.5-cm (1-inch) pieces. Set aside.
- Heat oil in a frying pan (skillet). Add chilli and brown sugar. Mix thoroughly.
- Add leeks and salt. Stir, then add tamarind juice and coconut milk.
- Cover pan and cook until leeks are tender. Serve warm.

Opposite: Sambal Goreng Prei

Pare-pare ⁓

(Stuffed Bitter Gourd)

Ingredients

Bitter gourds	2, medium
Minced (ground) pork	225 g (7½ oz)
Onion	1, peeled and chopped
Garlic	2 cloves, peeled and chopped
Light soy sauce (*kecap asin*)	3 Tbsp
Vegetable oil	2 Tbsp
Water	250 ml (1 cup)

Method

- Cut off one end of each bitter gourd and remove seeds. Parboil cleaned gourds for 10–15 minutes, then remove and leave to cool.
- In a bowl, combine pork, onion, garlic and soy sauce. Then, stuff mixture into bitter gourds.
- Heat oil and fry stuffed bitter gourds on both sides until light brown.
- Add water, cover tightly and cook for 30–40 minutes over medium heat. Serve.

Sweet and Sour Aubergines ⁓

Ingredients

Asian aubergine (eggplant/brinjal)	1, about 22-cm (9-inches) long
Sea salt	about 2 Tbsp
Freshly ground black pepper	about 2 Tbsp
Vegetable oil	3 Tbsp
Butter or margarine	1 Tbsp
Onion	1, medium, peeled and chopped
Sweet soy sauce (*kecap manis*)	2 Tbsp
Tamarind pulp (*asam Jawa*)	1 Tbsp
Water	125 ml (½ cup)

Method

- Slice Asian aubergine into 7.5-cm lengths (3-inch), then halve each length. Diagonally score each cut side in both directions, resulting in diamond shapes.
- Sprinkle salt and pepper on scored surfaces. Alternatively, mix salt and pepper in a shallow dish and dip aubergine pieces, scored side down, into mixture.
- Over medium heat, heat oil in a heavy frying pan (skillet) until hot but not smoking.
- Sauté aubergine pieces in batches, scored side down first, then brown skins. Drain on absorbent paper towels.
- Wipe pan clean and over medium heat, melt butter or margarine.
- Sauté onion until softened but not browned. Then, add soy sauce, tamarind and water. Bring to a simmer.
- Add aubergine pieces, skin side down. Spoon sauce over tops.
- Reduce heat, cover tightly and simmer for 5 minutes. Serve.

Opposite: Pare-pare

Gado-gado ✑
(Indonesian Salad)

Ingredients

Firm bean curd	1 piece
Vegetable oil	1 tsp
Cabbage	1, small, coarsely chopped and boiled
String beans	225 g (7½ oz), strings removed, halved and boiled
Spinach	225 g (7½ oz), parboiled
Watercress	1 bunch, parboiled
Bean sprouts	225 g (7½ oz), tailed if desired and scalded
Cucumber	1, small, peeled and sliced
Eggs	2, hard-boiled, shelled and quartered
Prawn (shrimp) crackers	

Method

- Sauté bean curd in vegetable oil until brown. When cool, slice into bite-size portions.
- Onto each serving dish, put desired amounts of cabbage, beans, spinach, watercress and bean sprouts. Garnish with cucumber, eggs, bean curd and crumbled prawn crackers.
- Serve Gado-gado with peanut sauce (see next recipe), either poured over the dish or, if preferred, separately.

Gado-gado Saus Kacang ✑
(Gado-gado Peanut Sauce)

Ingredients

Cooking oil	1 Tbsp
Onion	1, peeled and chopped
Garlic	1 clove, peeled and chopped
Creamy or crunchy peanut butter	4 Tbsp
Water	125 ml (½ cup)
Green chillies	3, crushed
Lemon grass (*serai*)	a pinch, ground
Brown sugar	1 tsp
Dried prawn (shrimp) paste (*terasi*)	1 pea-size piece
Tamarind (*asam Jawa*) juice (see pg 16)	1 Tbsp
Sweet soy sauce (*kecap manis*)	1 tsp
Salt	1 tsp
Coconut milk	125 ml (½ cup), squeezed from ¼ grated coconut with sufficient water added

Method

- Heat oil and fry onion and garlic. Set aside.
- Mix peanut butter with water and bring to the boil. Remove from heat and add chillies, lemon grass, brown sugar, dried prawn paste, tamarind juice, soy sauce and salt.
- Add in onion and garlic and mix thoroughly.
- Stir in coconut milk and when the mixture is smooth, simmer over low heat until heated through. Serve atop Gado-gado or separately in a gravy boat.

NOTE: If a spicy-hot sauce is preferred, simply increase the amount of chillies.

Homemade Tempe ～⁀o

(Fermented Soy Bean Cakes)

Although you can easily buy ready-made *tempe*, there's nothing like the real, homemade version. Because *tempe* is fermented and 'alive', the pasteurisation process, at least for my daughter, 'kills' not only the germs, but also the taste. To my daughter, homemade *tempe* is well worth the work. I want to thank Titi Ronodipuro for this recipe.

Ingredients

Soy beans (white)	225 g (1 cup)
Rice yeast (*ragi*)	3 tablets, see note
Water	
White vinegar	
Aluminium foil or banana leaves	

Method

- Put soy beans into a large pasta pot. Add sufficient water to cover beans and boil as you would pasta for 20 minutes. Drain.
- 'Peel' soy beans by soaking in tap water and squeezing to remove outer skins. Transfer peeled soy beans to a large ceramic bowl.
- Add sufficient water-vinegar solution to cover peeled beans; to make solution, mix 1 part white vinegar with 10 parts water. Leave beans to soak for at least 4 hours.
- Meanwhile, cut aluminium foil or banana leaves into 15-cm (6-inch) squares, 12–15 pieces should suffice.
- At the end of soaking, bring beans and water-vinegar solution to the boil. Drain.
- Cool beans quickly by fanning and constantly stirring with a wooden spoon. From this point on, do not touch beans with hands.
- Add rice yeast to beans and mix well with a wooden spoon.
- Spoon sufficient mixture onto the centre of each foil square. Fold foil up tightly around beans so that no air can get in.

- Keep foil packets for at least 48 hours in temperatures of 24°C/75°F or warmer. Do not place packets in a gas oven because fumes from the pilot light will kill the rice yeast.
- To test the fermentation process, open 1 packet. The resulting *tempe* should look like a web-like cocoon and the beans will not easily separate.
- Once-used foil can be saved for the same purpose in future — the rice yeast will continue in minute quantities and the fermentation process will take less time.

NOTE: This recipe assumes the use of rice yeast tablets that are sold in 50-gram bags, each containing 20 tablets.

Sawi Asin ～⁀o

(Salted Greens)

Ingredients

Chinese flowering cabbage

Salt

Rice water

Method

- Wash flowering cabbage thoroughly.
- Take a generous amount of salt and bruise the stalks, making sure that salt reaches all parts. Make small bundles and tie with strings. Put into a crock or glass jar.
- Before cooking rice for the next meal, be mindful to reserve rice water. Wash rice in a basin with a large amount of water. Pour resulting chalky liquid over vegetable bunches and be sure they are completely immersed.
- The pickled greens should be ready in 4 or 5 days; they go well mixed with cooked pork.

Corn Fritters with Prawns ✦

Ingredients

Fresh corn	3 ears
Sea salt	½ tsp
Spring onions (scallions)	2, finely chopped
Prawns (shrimps)	8–10, medium-size, peeled and minced
Egg	1, medium-size
Plain (all-purpose) flour	3 tsp
Ground white pepper	a dash
Cooking oil	1 Tbsp
Butter or margarine	2 Tbsp

Method

- Grate corn coarsely with the back of a knife to remove kernels, then transfer to a bowl. Add salt, spring onions, prawns, egg, flour and pepper. Mix well.
- In a heavy frying pan (skillet), heat oil and butter until bubbling hot, then reduce heat.
- Spoon 6 Tbsp of batter, one at a time, onto pan. Take care that fritters do not touch. Allow to cook for 4–5 minutes or until set and slightly brown. To check, gently lift the side of fritter with a blunt knife.
- Flip fritters with a spatula and cook other sides, about 3 minutes.
- Remove fritters when cooked through and drain on absorbent paper towels.

NOTE: The fritters can be made beforehand and warmed in the oven before serving.

Cap Cai Ca ✦
(Mixed Vegetables, Sino-Indonesian Style)

Ingredients

Lean pork chop	1, boned and diced
Water	375 ml (1½ cups)
Salt	1 tsp
Chicken breast	1, about 360 g (12 oz)
Ginger	a pinch, ground
Peanut oil	2 Tbsp
Onion	1, medium, peeled and chopped
Garlic	2 cloves, peeled and chopped
Fresh or frozen prawns (shrimps)	225 g (7½ oz), peeled
Light soy sauce (*kecap asin*)	1 Tbsp
Cabbage	1, small, coarsely chopped
Leeks	2, coarsely chopped
Corn flour (cornstarch)	2 tsp, dissolved in 3 Tbsp water

Method

- Put pork into a saucepan, add 125 ml (½ cup) water and ½ tsp salt. Cover, bring to the boil and simmer until cooked. Remove from heat and leave pork to cool in cooking liquid to prevent drying out.
- Put chicken into a clean saucepan. Add remaining water and salt, as well as ginger. Cook until tender. Remove chicken and dice. Reserve chicken bouillon.
- In a larger pan, heat oil and add onion and garlic. Sauté lightly.
- Add cooked pork and chicken, prawns and soy sauce. Mix thoroughly.
- Pour in chicken bouillon and bring to the boil. Then, add cabbage and leeks and cook for only a few minutes so vegetables retain crispness.
- Finally, add corn flour solution and return to the boil. Remove and serve.
- With white rice and some crushed red chillies, this dish constitutes a meal in itself.

Opposite: Cap Cai Ca

Eggs

It is said of the egg that perhaps no other single article of food can be used in so many intriguing ways. This is certainly borne out by the wide usage of eggs in both Occidental and Oriental cooking. In contemporary Asia, as in the West, the egg is considered a rich source of nutrition. Little wonder; nine eggs, the equivalent of 450 g (1 lb) in weight, has the nutritive value of 450 g of beef. Thus, in impoverished lands, the egg is often a substitute for meat, although the poverty of some areas is so deep that people prefer to raise fowls and sell rather than consume their poultry and its by-product.

In Indonesia, on the main islands of Java, Sumatra and Sulawesi, and along the tiny bracelet of islands embracing Bali, known as the Nusa Tenggara chain, domesticated fowl is plentiful and, therefore, so are eggs. Every village maintains its own flock of chickens, ducks or geese; the last do double-duty as sentries at night, creating an awful din should anyone approach the village. However, if you are from a Western background and are accustomed to chicken's eggs, it would be wise in Indonesia to specify chicken's eggs (*telur ayam*) in a restaurant or hotel. Otherwise, the likelihood is that you will be served a slightly rubbery egg with a hard yellow yolk and bluish colouring — a duck's egg. Indonesians prize the duck's egg with cause.

Although the Javanese are often portrayed as abstruse, they also have an earth-bound, practical side. Indonesians prefer the duck's egg simply because it is larger than the chicken's egg and you can, therefore, get more nourishment from it. Nobody can argue with such realism but having been accustomed to chicken's eggs, I find that it requires stoic discipline and the reorientation of prejudices to sit down to a plate of duck's eggs. Baking, of course, is another story. In the United States, duck's eggs are the favourite of the commercial baker and for the same reason that the Indonesian farmer is impressed. This disingenuity is not confined solely to the Western world; the Chinese are also rather cool to duck's eggs and most Chinese restaurants hide them in their superb soups. The diner is unaware of this, of course, and nobody can argue with Chinese soup — the world's finest — particularly the fabulous melon and asparagus and crab-egg soups of Glodok, Jakarta's Chinese quarter.

While the following Indonesian egg recipes invariably call for duck's eggs, chicken's eggs, white or brown and preferably in the smaller-graded size, can be used in all recipes except the first (Telur Asin).

Telur Asin ✦

(Salted Eggs)

Ingredients

Duck's eggs	10
Water	2 litres (8 cups / 3¹/₅ pints)
Coarse salt	450 g (1 lb)
Saltpetre (potassium nitrate)	½ tsp

Method

- Put eggs into an old-fashioned earthen jar or bean pot.
- Bring water to the boil in a pot. Dissolve salt and saltpetre in boiling water, then remove from heat and leave to cool.
- Pour cooled solution over eggs and store for 3 weeks.
- When required, remove eggs from earthen jar or bean pot and hard-boil them.
- To serve, slice each egg in half, but retain shell.

Dadar Tegal ✦

(Omelette Tegal)

Ingredients

Eggs	5
Spring onion (scallion)	1, coarsely chopped
Dried prawn (shrimp) paste (*terasi*)	1 pea-size piece, softened in 1 tsp water
Salt	½ tsp
Peanut oil	2 Tbsp

Method

- Crack eggs into a bowl and beat lightly. Add spring onion, dried prawn paste and salt. Stir.
- Heat peanut oil in a frying pan (skillet). Pour in egg mixture and fry on both sides.
- Cut omelette into broad strips and serve warm.

Opposite: Dadar Tegal

Telur Dadar ❧

(Simple Omelette)

Ingredients

Onion	1, medium, peeled and finely chopped
Red chilli	1, medium, thinly sliced
Peanut oil	1 Tbsp
Eggs	5
Salt	½ tsp
Vegetable oil or margarine	2 Tbsp

Method

- Fry onion and chilli in peanut oil until onion is earthy brown. Dish out and set aside.
- Crack eggs into a bowl and beat lightly. Mix in salt.
- Heat oil or margarine in a clean frying pan (skillet). Pour in eggs and as omelette settles, sprinkle lightly with fried onion-chilli combination, which gives the omelette a wonderful flavour. Turn omelette over and do the same with the other side.
- Cut cooked omelette into narrow strips and serve warm.

Dadar Udang ❧

(Prawn Omelette)

Ingredients

Fresh or frozen prawns (shrimps)	200 g (1 cup)
Plain (all-purpose) flour	1 Tbsp
Milk	3 Tbsp
Eggs	6
Nutmeg (*pala*)	a pinch, ground
Ground black pepper	a pinch
Salt	1 tsp
Vegetable oil or margarine	3 Tbsp
Parsley	1 Tbsp, chopped

Method

- Peel and devein prawns, then chop until fine.
- Mix flour with milk. Set batter aside.
- Crack eggs into a bowl and beat lightly. Add batter to eggs and mix well. Then, add nutmeg, pepper and salt. Stir to mix, then add prawns.
- Heat oil or margarine in a clean frying pan (skillet). Make an omelette of egg mixture and cut into broad strips. Sprinkle with parsley and serve warm.

Sambal Goreng Telur ～

(Spiced Eggs)

Ingredients

Eggs	5, hard-boiled, shelled and halved
Peanut oil	2 Tbsp
Onion	1, medium, peeled and chopped
Garlic	2 cloves, peeled and chopped
Candlenut (*kemiri*)	1, grated
Galangal (*laos*)	1 tsp
Sambal oelek (see pg 159)	1 tsp
Salt	to taste
Brown sugar	½ tsp
Salam leaf (*daun salam*)	1
Coconut milk	250 ml (1 cup), squeezed from ½ grated coconut with sufficient water added

Method

- Arrange egg halves on a serving dish. Set aside.
- Heat oil in a saucepan. Sauté onion, garlic, candlenut, galangal, *sambal oelek* and salt. Be cautious to avoid burning.
- Add brown sugar, *salam* leaf and coconut milk. Bring to the boil, then simmer for 10 minutes.
- Pour mixture over hard-boiled eggs and serve. Alternatively, lower eggs into the spice mixture and heat together for a few minutes before serving.

Dadar Jawa ∾

(Omelette Java)

Ingredients

Eggs	5
Spring onion (scallion)	1, finely chopped
Dried prawn (shrimp) paste (*terasi*)	1 pea-size piece, softened in 1 tsp water
Sambal oelek (see pg 159)	½ tsp
Tamarind (*asam Jawa*) juice (see pg 16)	a dash
Salt	½ tsp
Vegetable oil or margarine	2 Tbsp

Method

- Crack eggs into a bowl and beat lightly.
- Add spring onion, dried prawn paste, *sambal oelek*, tamarind juice and salt. Stir to combine.
- Heat oil or margarine in a frying pan (skillet). Pour in egg mixture and fry on both sides.
- Cut resulting omelette into wide strips. Serve.

Telur Kari ∾

(Curried Eggs)

Ingredients

Peanut oil	2 Tbsp
Onion	1, medium, peeled and chopped
Garlic	1 clove, peeled and chopped
Curry powder	2 tsp or more to taste
Lemon grass (*serai*)	½ tsp, ground
Sambal oelek (see pg 159)	1 tsp
Salam leaf (*daun salam*)	1
Kaffir lime leaf (*daun jeruk purut*)	1
Coconut milk	375 ml (1½ cups), squeezed from ½ grated coconut with sufficient water added
Salt	1 tsp
Eggs	6, hard-boiled and shelled

Method

- Heat oil in a frying pan (skillet). Add chopped onion and garlic, as well as curry powder and mix well. Fry lightly.
- Add lemon grass, *sambal oelek*, *salam* leaf, kaffir lime leaf, coconut milk and salt. Bring to the boil.
- Add eggs and simmer for 10 minutes. Serve.

Opposite: Telur Kari

Some Indonesian dishes defy classification, yet are integral parts of any rice table. Indeed, they are delicacies in themselves and are certain to whet the appreciative Western appetite. These dishes run the gamut from *krupuk* and *lumpia goreng* to *pisang goreng* and *bahmi*.

Krupuk, which is easily prepared, is a thin, light-weight, prawn (shrimp) or fish cracker, somewhat similar to the American potato chip but made from a prawn (shrimp) base. A *rijsttafel* is invariably garnished with a few *krupuk* crackers, so is almost any other Indonesian meal. On the cocktail circuit, perhaps needless to observe, they perform wonderfully as a titbit. Another favourite is *lumpia goreng*, a distant but discernible relative of the Chinese spring roll (erroneously but popularly called an egg roll by most Westerners). *Lumpia* is often served as an appetiser, accompanied by a ginger sauce. Most assuredly, Indonesia's version is Chinese in origin.

Another unclassified delight is *pisang goreng* or sautéed bananas prepared in the uncoated West Indies style. The Indonesians also deep-fry them with a coating of flour and egg batter, as is the custom in South America. In Indonesia, sautéed bananas should not be eaten during the meal but in the colonial period, the Dutch considered a *rijsttafel* incomplete without sautéed bananas and the idea has gradually taken hold.

Europeanised hotels and restaurants now usually serve them with the main meal and the custom is spreading. Little wonder, too, they contribute a marvellous flavour and act as a mild chutney in cooling the palate and providing a contrast to the hotly spiced side-dishes.

In this loose category of odds and ends, I have deliberately placed *bahmi* or noodle dishes, although purists will complain that they constitute a classification, if not a book, in themselves. I concede this point in Chinese or Vietnamese cookery but not when it comes to Indonesian even though *bahmi*, which is an inexpensive, filling and nourishing dish, has assumed a prominent place in the average diet. Indonesian *bahmi* dishes are variations on a Chinese theme. They are not served at a rice table but constitute meals in themselves. Like Italian noodles, which Marco Polo introduced to Genoa after his return from Cathay and the islands of silver (Sumatra) and gold (Java), *bahmi* comes in different lengths and widths. Several popular *bahmi* dishes follow in this section in recognition that a volume on Indonesian cooking would be incomplete without them, although *bahmi* is not an authentic Indonesian dish. Perhaps that statement is debatable. Is spaghetti an authentic Italian dish? The Italians would most assuredly claim it is.

Odds and Ends

Serundeng ∾
(Coconut-peanut Garnish)

Ingredients

Vegetable oil	1 Tbsp
Onion	1, medium, peeled and sliced
Garlic	3 cloves, peeled and chopped
Coriander (*ketumbar*)	½ tsp, ground
Cumin (*jintan*)	a pinch, ground
Galangal (*laos*)	½ tsp, ground
Dried prawn (shrimp) paste (*terasi*)	1 pea-size piece
Brown sugar	1 tsp
Salam leaf (*daun salam*)	1
Salt	1 tsp
Coconut	1 cup, desiccated or freshly grated
Roasted peanuts	100 g (½ cup), salted or unsalted

Method

- Heat oil in a frying pan (skillet). Add onion and garlic. Sauté lightly, then add coriander, cumin, galangal, dried prawn paste, brown sugar, *salam* leaf and salt. Stir well and keep heat low.
- Add coconut and toast ingredients, stirring continuously until coconut becomes an even, crisp, medium brown.
- Mix in roasted peanuts and fry for about 3 minutes. Then, remove from heat, leave to cool and serve as a *rijsttafel* garnish.

Rempah Kelapa ∾
(Spicy Coconut Balls)

Ingredients

Coconut	1 cup, desiccated or freshly grated
Garlic	2 cloves, peeled and chopped
Eggs	2
Plain (all-purpose) flour	1 Tbsp
Tamarind (*asam Jawa*) juice (see pg 16)	1 Tbsp
Lemon grass (*serai*)	½ tsp, ground
Coriander (*ketumbar*)	½ tsp, ground
Galangal (*laos*)	½ tsp, ground
Turmeric (*kunyit*)	a pinch, ground
Sugar	a pinch
Salam leaf (*daun salam*)	1, crushed
Dried prawn (shrimp) paste (*terasi*)	1 pea-size piece
Salt	1 tsp
Vegetable oil for deep-frying	

Method

- Except oil, mix all other ingredients thoroughly in a bowl. Shape tiny balls from resulting mixture, about the size of pigeon eggs.
- Heat sufficient oil for deep-frying until hot. Deep-fry several balls at a time until deep brown. Serve as a *rijsttafel* garnish.

Opposite: Rempah Kelapa

Krupuk Udang ⌛
(Prawn Crackers)

Ingredients

Vegetable oil	500 ml (2 cups)
Uncooked prawn crackers	24 pieces

Method

- Heat oil in a heavy frying pan (skillet) until hot.
- Fry crackers one at a time. In the frying process, the dainty crackers will treble in size. Stir continuously during frying and remove with a slotted spoon.
- Drain crackers on absorbent paper towels. Serve hot or cold, as desired.

NOTE: Melinjo wafers or *emping* has the consistency of prawn crackers and is white in appearance. The cracker is the roasted fruit of the tropical melinjo tree and has a delightful taste, almost like burnt almond. It is cooked in the same fashion as prawn crackers but sprinkled with salt before serving.

Rempeyeh ⌛
(Peanut Fritter)

Ingredients

Rice flour	120 g (1 cup)
Coconut milk	250 ml (1 cup)
Coriander (*ketumbar*)	½ tsp, ground
Salt	½ tsp
Garlic	1 clove, peeled and chopped
Cumin (*jintan*)	a pinch, ground
Turmeric (*kunyit*)	a pinch, ground
Candlenut (*kemiri*)	1, grated
Raw peanuts	100 g (½ cup)
Cooking oil for deep-frying	

Method

- Mix rice flour with coconut milk. Then, add coriander, salt, garlic, cumin, turmeric and candlenut. Mix well.
- Add in raw peanuts; the batter will be on the watery side.
- Heat sufficient oil for deep-frying. Fry batter by the tablespoon until golden brown. Remove and drain on absorbent paper towels. Serve.
- The *rempeyeh* will be like flat, thin crunchy wafers.

Opposite: Rempeyeh

Bahmi Goreng Ayam ✎

(Chicken and Noodles)

Ingredients

Egg noodles	225 g (7½ oz)
Chicken breast	1
Garlic	3 cloves, peeled and chopped
Vegetable oil	3 Tbsp
Light or dark soy sauce	1 Tbsp
Cabbage leaves	3, thinly cut
Salt	to taste
Spring onion (scallion)	1, sliced
Prawns (shrimps)	225 g (7½ oz), peeled and cooked

Method

- Bring sufficient water for cooking noodles to the boil in a pot. Lower in noodles and cook for 1 minute or until tender. Remove and run noodles under cold tap water. Drain using a strainer and set aside.
- Remove meat from chicken breast and dice. Lightly fry diced chicken and garlic in oil in a heavy frying pan (skillet).
- Add soy sauce, stir well and fry for 1 minute, then add cabbage and fry until cabbage wilts.
- Add cooked noodles and salt to taste. Stir-fry continuously, cooking over low heat. Then, add spring onion and fry for about 2 minutes.
- Mix in cooked prawns and heat mixture for 2 minutes more, still stirring frequently.
- Remove noodles to an oval platter. If desired, garnish with a thinly sliced plain omelette or crisp-fried shallots.

NOTE: Bahmi Goreng Babi (Pork and Noodles) and Bahmi Goreng Sapi (Beef and Noodles) may be cooked in the same manner using pork and beef respectively instead of chicken. It is also common to mix chicken, pork, shrimps and crabmeat together in any combination.

Bahmi Goreng sama Udang ✎

(Prawns and Noodles)

Ingredients

Egg noodles	450 g (1 lb)
Fresh prawns (shrimps)	450 g (1 lb), peeled
Vegetable oil	2 Tbsp
Onion	1, medium, peeled and sliced
Garlic	2 cloves, peeled and chopped
Light soy sauce	1 Tbsp
Chicken bouillon (stock) cube	1, dissolved in 250 ml (1 cup) hot water
Spring onions (scallions)	3, thinly cut

Method

- Bring sufficient water for cooking noodles to the boil. Lower in noodles and cook for 1 minute or until tender. Then, remove and run under cold tap water. Drain cooled noodles with a strainer.
- In a heavy frying pan (skillet), fry prawns in oil for about 5 minutes.
- Add onion and garlic to prawns and fry until onion slices turn medium brown.
- Add soy sauce and cooked noodles, mixing thoroughly.
- While frying, splash in small amounts of bouillon to prevent noodle mixture from burning and pan-sticking. Reserve unused bouillon for future use.
- Finally, mix in scallions and fry until dry but avoid burning. Remove to an oval-shaped platter.
- This dish constitutes a meal in itself and can be garnished with a plain omelette sliced into thin strips, and with parsley.

Pancit Goreng ❧

Ingredients

Minced (ground) pork or chicken	450 g (1 lb)
Garlic	2 cloves, peeled and minced
Light soy sauce (*kecap asin*)	1½ Tbsp or to taste
Wonton skins	1 package (450 g)
Eggs	2, lightly beaten
Cooking oil for deep-frying	

Method

- In a dry and heavy frying pan (skillet), fry pork and garlic over medium heat until pork is crumbly and no longer pink, about 10 minutes.
- Add soy sauce and mix well. Then, remove from heat and leave to cool completely.
- Prepare *pancit*. Take a wonton skin and position it with one point facing you.
- Spoon a small quantity (a scant teaspoon) of meat mixture onto the centre of skin.
- Dip your fingers into the beaten egg, then moisten all 4 sides of wonton skin.
- Working quickly, bring point closest to you to the point furthest to you. You have now made a triangle, with the longest side facing you. Press 2 sides of triangle together.
- Take points on left and right and bring together, making a little 'hat'. Dab a little beaten egg on the tips and press to seal. Repeat until ingredients are used up; meat mixture should make about 36 *pancit*.
- Heat sufficient oil for deep-frying, then lower *pancit* into oil and fry until golden.
- Drain on absorbent paper towels.

NOTE: *Pancit* can be made beforehand and warmed on a baking tray in an oven preheated to 175°C/350°F for about 5 minutes. A splendid array of dipping sauces, mild and spicy can be served alongside Pancit Goreng. Thai chilli sauces, readily available, and peanut sauce make good dips.

Bihun ❧
(Chicken and Rice Vermicelli)

Ingredients

Dried rice vermicelli (*bihun*)	1 package, about 240 g (8 oz)
Spring onions (scallions)	2, cut into 2.5-cm (1-inch) lengths
Coconut milk	1 can (400 ml)
Salam leaf (*daun salam*)	1
Coriander (*ketumbar*)	1 tsp, ground
Lemon grass (*serai*)	1 stalk, crushed
Chicken breast	1, boned and cut into small cubes
Salt	1½ tsp or to taste
Sugar	a dash or to taste
Chives or coriander leaves (cilantro) for garnishing	

Method

- Cook vermicelli according to package directions. When done, stop cooking process by draining vermicelli in kitchen sink and washing with cold water. Transfer vermicelli to a large bowl of cold water.
- Into a large saucepan, put spring onions, coconut milk (with sufficient water added to make 500 ml (2 cups), *salam* leaf, coriander and lemon grass. Bring to the boil.
- Reduce heat and add chicken. Simmer for 8 minutes. Add salt and sugar to taste. Then, add drained vermicelli and bring to a simmer.
- Transfer to a large serving bowl and garnish.

Lumpia Goreng ❧

(Fried Indonesian Spring Rolls)

This dish requires 3 separate stages of preparation: 1) the filling, 2) the wrapping and 3) the sauce. In Indonesia, Lumpia Goreng is often served as an appetiser, while in the West, it also makes a fine cocktail snack.

Filling

Chicken breast	1, small, skinned if desired
Vegetable oil	2 Tbsp
Fresh prawns (shrimps)	about 120 g (½ cup), peeled and chopped
Garlic	2 cloves, peeled and chopped
Sweet soy sauce (*kecap manis*)	1 Tbsp
Cabbage leaves	3, use inner leaves, finely shredded
Bean sprouts	1 cup, tailed if desired
Spring onions (scallions)	2, chopped
Salt	to taste

Method

- Remove meat from chicken breast and dice.
- Fry diced chicken in oil in a heavy frying pan (skillet) for about 5 minutes.
- Add prawns to pan and fry 3 minutes.
- Add garlic and fry until light brown. Then, add soy sauce and stir well.
- Add cabbage and stir well, then add bean sprouts and mix thoroughly.
- Finally, add spring onions and cook over low heat for a few minutes until cabbage appears slightly wilted.
- Remove from heat and leave to cool completely. While filling is cooling, prepare wrapping.

Wrapping

Egg	1
Butter or margarine	2 Tbsp, melted
Salt	½ tsp
Plain (all-purpose) flour	120 g (1 cup)
Water	
Cooking oil for deep-frying	

Method

- Crack egg into a bowl and beat lightly. Add melted butter or margarine, stir well and add salt. Mix in flour as though making a pie crust. Add sufficient water to make a dough.
- Drop a tablespoon of dough at a time onto a floured board and roll out as thinly as possible. The pastry wrapping is now ready for filling.
- Put sufficient filling onto each piece of dough. Fold in left and right sides and roll up. Seal end with water or beaten egg white.
- Deep-fry rolls until light brown. Serve with ginger sauce (see recipe below) or hot English mustard.

NOTE: To save time, use ready-made spring roll wrappers, either fresh or frozen, instead.

Sauce

Sambal oelek (see pg 159)	½ tsp
Chopped ginger	a pinch
Sugar	1 tsp
Corn flour (cornstarch)	1 tsp
Dark soy sauce	1 tsp
Tamarind (*asam Jawa*) juice (see pg 16)	1 Tbsp
Water	3 Tbsp

Method

- Mix all ingredients together in a small saucepan. Stir thoroughly and cook over low heat until sauce thickens. Serve.

NOTE: A shorter and simpler method would be to mix together 4 Tbsp apricot jam, a pinch of chopped ginger and 2 Tbsp light soy sauce (*kecap asin*).

Opposite: Lumpia Goreng

Telo ~

(Savoury Snack)

As a child, this was one of my favourite savoury snacks. It came in a banana leaf pouch and consisted of a lightly browned *ubi kayu* (cassava/tapioca), dried fish (*ikan teri*, e.g., dried anchovies), onions and red chillies. My daughter prefers fresh prawns instead of dried fish or prawns. Whether you use dried prawns or fresh, this is a very spicy snack.

Ingredients

Fresh prawns (shrimps)	225 g (7½ oz), large, or 1 cup *ikan teri* (anchovies)
Cooking oil	1 Tbsp
Onion	1, medium, peeled and chopped
Garlic	1 clove, peeled and finely chopped
Tomato (optional)	1, small
Red chillies	1–3, sliced (for less heat, deseed)
Sweet soy sauce (*kecap manis*)	1 Tbsp
Light soy sauce (*kecap asin*)	1 Tbsp
Tapioca (cassava)	1, large, peeled, cut into 7.5-cm (3-inch) chunks and boiled in water until tender

Method

- If using fresh prawns, clean, peel and cut each prawn into 2. Set aside.
- In a frying pan (skillet), heat oil and sweat onion, garlic and tomato, if using. Do not brown.
- Add chillies and prawns or *ikan teri*. Mix well, then add soy sauces. Add a little water to prevent drying, if necessary.
- Cook over medium heat until prawns are pink or dried fish is heated through.

NOTE: Throughout the summer in New England, I grow a variety of hot peppers. At the end of the summer, I harvest them. Some I dry in an unlit oven for future use; others I pack in vinegar in jars and refrigerate. Still others I put in freezer bags and freeze. The pepper leaves at the end of the season are stir-fried with garlic and a little *terasi* (dried prawn (shrimp) paste) and are not only delicious, but also full of vitamins.

Vegetarian Lumpia ✍

Lumpia skins are available in most supermarkets. Sometimes, they are called egg roll wrappers or spring roll wrappers. The skins can be either thick or thin. I prefer the thicker skins because I think that they are easier to work with but my daughter likes the thinner ones and says that they are lighter and crispier when cooked.

Ingredients

Cooking oil	2 Tbsp and enough for deep-frying
Garlic	2 cloves, peeled and finely chopped
Cabbage	about 600 g (4 cups), thinly sliced
Yam bean (jicama)	about 200 g (½ cup), peeled and julienned
Snow peas	about 100 g (½ cup), julienned
Light soy sauce (*kecap asin*)	2 Tbsp
Spring roll skins	1 package, about 25 skins
Egg	1, beaten
Salt	
Spring onions (scallions)	2, thinly sliced

Method

- Heat 2 Tbsp oil in a frying pan (skillet) over medium heat. Sauté garlic until softened, but not browned.
- Add cabbage and cook until wilted, takes about 5 minutes.
- Add yam bean and snow peas. Mix well, then turn off heat and add soy sauce.
- Transfer vegetables to a colander to drain. Leave to cool completely.
- Cut spring roll skins in half diagonally so triangles result.
- Prepare rolls. Position 1 triangular skin so that one point faces away from you, and longest edge is nearest to you.
- Spoon 1 Tbsp cooled vegetable mixture along lower length of skin, flattening it to make a small log.
- The idea is to make an envelope: moisten a finger with beaten egg and run it along lower edge, then fold in both corners towards bottom centre and press to secure.
- Moisten edges of upper skin and tightly roll up to seal. Repeat until ingredients are used up.
- Heat sufficient oil for deep-frying and cook *lumpia* until brown. This recipe makes small *lumpia* that can be eaten out of hand.

NOTE: Yam bean or jicama is a very versatile root, with a sweet and crisp flavour. I use it in place of fresh water chestnuts. It is easier to peel and has a very long shelf life. For Rujak Buah-buah Pedes (Hot Fruit Chutney) on pg 170, you can substitute the pears and apples with yam bean.

Condiments

In the realm of condiments, the unbridled Indonesian imagination runs riot. Dozens of variations on a theme may appear on the rice table simultaneously. At this point, the problem for the hostess is to possess not one, but several lazy susans.

The variety of condiments available on the Indonesian islands puts to shame the appearance on the Western table of the standard salt and pepper shakers, Maggi or, in the case of the American, the ubiquitous ketchup bottle (sometimes spelt "catsup"). The word "ketchup", incidentally, is derived from the Malay word for soy sauce, *kecap*. In the West, of course, ketchup is wholly made from tomatoes.

Perhaps the most imaginative Indonesian garnish is *garam dan merica*, simply salt and pepper mixed together and served in a small dish instead of a shaker. Try it sometime, and not necessarily with Indonesian food. In Jarkata, and elsewhere in the archipelago, Chinese restaurants invariably serve this mixture with frog legs fried in butter. It makes for a magnificent snack and should be washed down with cold beer.

Western condiments are generally bland compared to the condiments found in the archipelago. To the uninitiated, the indiscriminate use of *sambals* will bring tears to the eyes and a burst of perspiration to the brow. Sometimes, though rarely, it even causes the initiated to cry — with joy, however.

As in the case of spices, not all Indonesian condiments or *sambals* are fiery hot. Several — particularly those involving the preparation of cucumbers, which may be served sliced and raw — are designed to cool the palate. These condiments assay a role similar to that of chutney in Indian cooking.

The preparation of *sambals* is complex but, fortunately, the growing popularity of Indonesian cooking has provided the cook with a short cut. Outside Southeast Asia, *sambals* may be purchased from importers of foreign foods.

Sambals are relatively inexpensive and come in small bottles. They are used sparingly with a meal, so do not let the profusion of different *sambals* frighten you. There are six basic ones, as follows:

sambal oelek — a fiery, crushed red chilli mixture whose thermostat has been raised by the addition of other hot spices.

sambal manis — a mild, sweet-tasting condiment.

sambal goreng — a popular blend of red chilli and other spices but dissimilar to *sambal oelek*.

sambal udang kering — a condiment made from prawn (shrimp) paste, a form commonly found in Thailand, Burma, Cambodia and, of course, Malaysia.

sambal peteh — a condiment made from the *peteh* bean which has an unusually strong and unpleasant odour, but which has a rare and tantalising taste.

sambal bajak — a fiery condiment which has a dull taste, and a delayed reaction.

Each of these *sambals* is used in the course of a *rijsttafel*, a dash at a time. Customarily, they are served either in a small dish or in the original bottle with a tiny spoon.

The *sambals* develop taste sensations wholly absent from Chinese, Western and Indian cookery.

Several types of *sambals*, however, can be easily prepared in the modern kitchen, requiring little more than a few spices and some cucumber, lemon, onion or coconut. The following recipes belong to this group. You will find that these relishes provide a new dimension to your adventures in eating.

Sambal Kecap

(Spiced Soy Sauce)

This dip is especially good with chicken dishes and all kinds of *satay*.

Ingredients

Red chillies	2, long
Dark soy sauce	3 Tbsp

Method

- Slice chillies into elongated strips and float in soy sauce. Serve in a condiment dish.
- For a less spicy taste, deseed chillies.

Sambal Jeruk

(Spicy Lemon)

Ingredients

Lemon	1
Red chillies	2, crushed
Dried prawn (shrimp) paste (*terasi*)	1 pea-size piece
Salt	1 tsp

Method

- Cut lemon into wafer-thin slices, then transfer to a serving bowl.
- Add chillies, dried prawn paste and salt. Mix thoroughly. Serve.

Sambal Kelapa

(Spicy Coconut)

Ingredients

Coconut	3 Tbsp, desiccated or freshly grated
Green chilli	1, crushed
Dried prawn (shrimp) paste (*terasi*)	1 pea-size piece
Galangal (*laos*)	½ tsp, ground
Salt	½ tsp
Vegetable oil	1 Tbsp

Method

- Sauté all ingredients in vegetable oil over medium heat, stirring constantly, until coconut appears to be turning light brown. Dish out and serve.

Opposite: Sambal Jeruk

Sambal Jelantah ✎

(Spiced Chillies with Prawn Paste)

Ingredients

Red chillies	4, finely chopped
Green chillies	4, finely chopped
Dried prawn (shrimp) paste (*terasi*)	1 tsp
Salt	½ tsp
Vegetable oil	1 Tbsp
Water	4 Tbsp

Method

- Sauté chillies, dried prawn paste and salt in vegetable oil for about 2 minutes.
- Add water and simmer over low heat until liquid is halved. Dish out onto a condiment dish and serve.

NOTE: If fresh chillies are not available, dried crushed chillies may be substituted.

Sambal Ketimun ✎

(Spicy Cucumber)

This is an important *rijsttafel* dish, for it cools and soothes the palate.

Ingredients

Cucumber	1, large
Candlenuts (*kemiri*)	2, grated
Red chillies	2, crushed
Dried prawn (shrimp) paste (*terasi*)	1 pea-size piece
Vinegar	60 ml (¼ cup)
Water	60 ml (¼ cup)
Salt	½ tsp

Method

- Peel cucumber, if desired, then slice into thin strips. Set aside.
- Put candlenuts into a serving bowl and add chillies, dried prawn paste, vinegar, water and salt. Stir well.
- Float cucumber strips on mixture and serve.

Opposite: Sambal Ketimun

Sambal Oelek ✒

(Chillies and Spices)

This mixture is an ingredient in most Indonesian dishes. A large quantity can be prepared and kept in the refrigerator for several weeks.

Ingredients

Red chillies	12
Dried prawn (shrimp) paste (*terasi*)	½ tsp
Salt	½ tsp
Tamarind (*asam Jawa*) juice (see pg 16)	1 Tbsp

Method

- Pound chillies, dried prawn paste and salt together using a mortar and pestle. Alternatively, combine in a blender (processor). Transfer to a container.
- Stir in tamarind juice and serve.

Sambal Bajak ✒

(Fried Spicy Chillies)

Ingredients

Onion	1, medium, finely chopped
Garlic	6 cloves, peeled and finely chopped
Vegetable oil	1 Tbsp
Red chillies	3, crushed
Salt	1 tsp
Brown sugar	1 Tbsp
Candlenuts (*kemiri*)	12, grated
Galangal (*laos*)	½ tsp, ground
Dried prawn (shrimp) paste (*terasi*)	1 tsp
Salam leaves (*daun salam*)	2
Lemon grass (*serai*)	1 stalk
Kaffir lime leaves (*daun jeruk purut*)	2
Tamarind (*asam Jawa*) juice (see pg 16)	1 Tbsp
Water	6 Tbsp

Method

- Sauté onion and garlic in vegetable oil until light brown.
- Add chillies, salt and brown sugar. Fry for about 2 minutes.
- Add candlenuts, galangal, dried prawn paste, *salam* leaves, lemon grass, kaffir lime leaves and tamarind juice. Stir well for several minutes.
- Add water and simmer over low heat until almost dry. Remove from heat and leave to cool.
- Transfer to a jar after removing leaves. *Sambal bajak* can be kept for a very long period.

Opposite: Sambal Oelek

Relishes

No *rijsttafel*, or for that matter Asian dinner, is complete without an array of relishes and/or pickles. Relishes, like the tributaries of a river, feed the mainstream. They add zest to any dinner and "zest", according to both the Oxford and Webster dictionaries, is something which enhances a pleasant taste. Coincidentally, of course, the relish imparts a taste of its own.

In the West, relishes are normally piquant. In Southeast Asia, they run the gamut from searingly spicy to pungently sweet. On the islands, however, *acars* or relishes are invariably mild. They tend to complement the hot dishes prepared with *sambal goreng*. *Acars* alert the palate for the next round.

Indonesia's relishes are different and easy to prepare. They are often made several days in advance and may be stored for a considerable length of time under routine refrigeration. With an Indonesian meal, *acars* are a must. In the West, they are ideally suited to barbecues, with either American-style hamburgers or broiled steaks. One of the most popular brands of *acar* in Indonesia, a sort of household Heinz, is Mevr Kouw, a superb Sino-Indonesian mixture of pickled cauliflower, cucumbers, dill and so forth.

Ketimun ♠

(Cucumber)

Ingredients

Cucumbers	2, large

Method

- Peel cucumbers, then halve lengthways. Remove and discard pulpy cores. Slice remaining cucumbers into elongated strips.
- Serve cucumber slices cold as an accompaniment to spicy-hot main courses.

Acar Ketimun ♠

(Pickled Cucumber)

Ingredients

Cucumber	1, large
Vinegar	2 tsp
Water	125 ml (½ cup)
Salt	1 tsp
Red chilli	1, crushed

Method

- Peel cucumber, then cut into thin circular slices. Set aside.
- Mix vinegar, water and salt in a serving bowl. Float cucumber slices on liquid and sprinkle with chillies.
- Serve with rice dishes.

Acar Ketimun Jawa ♠

(Javanese Pickled Cucumber)

Ingredients

Cucumber	1, large
Salt	2 tsp
Water	60 ml (¼ cup)
Vinegar	85 ml (⅓ cup)
Granulated sugar	60 g (¼ cup)
Black peppercorns	3
Cloves (*cengkeh*)	3

Method

- Cube cucumber into bite-size portions and transfer to a Pyrex or similar dish. Set aside.
- Mix salt, water, vinegar, sugar, peppercorns and cloves in a saucepan and bring to a slow boil.
- Reduce heat and simmer for 5 minutes more.
- Pour cooked liquid over cucumber and leave to cool.
- Traditionally, cucumber cubes were put into an earthen pot with the cooked liquid poured over and left to stand for 3 days before serving.

Opposite: Acar Ketimun Jawa

Acar Biet ᷈

(Pickled Beets)

Ingredients

Beets	4
Cloves (*cengkeh*)	3
Black peppercorns	3
Brown sugar	1 Tbsp
Vinegar	85 ml (¹/₃ cup)
Water	85 ml (¹/₃ cup)

Method

- Boil beets in sufficient water until softened. Leave to cool, then peel and slice. Set aside.
- In a clean pot, bring all remaining ingredients to the boil. Simmer for 15 minutes.
- Pour cooked mixture over beets and leave to steep for at least 2 hours. Serve.

Acar Bawang Pedes ᷈

(Spicy Pickled Onion)

Ingredients

Onion	1, large, peeled and finely chopped
Tamarind (*asam Jawa*) juice (see pg 16)	4 Tbsp
Chilli (hot pepper) sauce	2 tsp

Method

- Mix all ingredients together and serve.

Acar Ketimun Kuning ᷈

(Yellow Pickled Cucumbers)

Ingredients

Cucumbers	3, large
Onion	1, small, peeled and finely chopped
Water	85 ml (¹/₃ cup)
Vinegar	60 ml (¼ cup)
Granulated sugar	60 g (¼ cup)
Cloves (*cengkeh*)	2
Chopped ginger	a pinch
Turmeric (*kunyit*)	1 tsp, ground
Salt	2 tsp

Method

- Peel cucumbers and halve lengthways. Remove and discard pulpy cores, then slice into bite-size portions.
- Transfer prepared cucumbers to a Pyrex or similar dish with a cover and set aside.
- Put onion into a saucepan and add water, vinegar, sugar, cloves, ginger, turmeric and salt. Bring to the boil and simmer for 15 minutes.
- Pour cooked liquid over cucumber and leave to cool.
- Cover dish and refrigerate for at least 4 hours before serving. Serve cold.

Opposite: Acar Bawang Pedes

Acar Bloemkool ~~

(Pickled Cauliflower)

Ingredients

Cauliflower	1 head, small
Turmeric (*kunyit*)	½ tsp, ground
Chopped ginger	a pinch
Vinegar	60 ml (¼ cup)
Garlic	1 clove, peeled
Water	85 ml (⅓ cup)
Granulated sugar	1 Tbsp
Salt	1 tsp

Method

- Cut or gently dismember cauliflower head into florets. Parboil florets and drain, then put into a deep dish with a cover.
- In a clean saucepan, bring all remaining ingredients to the boil. Pour resulting liquid over cauliflower. Leave to cool.
- Cover dish and let stand for at least 12 hours. Serve cool.

Acar Nanas ~~

(Pickled Pineapple)

Ingredients

Pineapple	1, small
Whole cloves (*cengkeh*)	
Vinegar	125 ml (½ cup)
Sugar	60 g (¼ cup)
Water	165 ml (⅔ cup)

Method

- Peel and core pineapple, then cut into serving portions.
- Tack a clove into each piece of pineapple. Transfer to an earthen bean or similar pot.
- Bring vinegar, sugar and water to a slow boil in a saucepan. Simmer for 10 minutes.
- Pour cooked liquid over prepared pineapple and leave to cool.
- Replace cover on pot and leave to pickle for at least 6 hours. Serve.

Opposite: Acar Nanas

Acar Buncis ✤
(Pickled String Beans)

Ingredients

String beans	450 g (1 lb), strings removed
Cloves (*cengkeh*)	3
Black peppercorns	3
Sambal oelek (see pg 159)	½ tsp
Water	125 ml (½ cup)
Granulated sugar	1 Tbsp
Salt	2 tsp
Vinegar	125 ml (½ cup)

Method

- Pack string beans upright in a mason or Pyrex jar. Add cloves, peppercorns and *sambal oelek*. Set aside.
- Bring water, sugar, salt and vinegar to the boil. Simmer for about 10 minutes, then pour liquid over beans.
- Replace cover on jar. Let stand for at least 3 days before serving.

Acar Bawang Timor ✤
(Pickled Onions)

Ingredients

White onions	12, small
Cooking oil	1 tsp
Candlenuts (*kemiri*)	3, grated
Ginger	a pinch, ground
Turmeric (*kunyit*)	a pinch, ground
Vinegar	125 ml (½ cup)
Water	250 ml (1 cup)
Salt	1 tsp

Method

- Peel onions, then wash and dry with absorbent paper towels. Put onions into an earthen bean pot or glass jar.
- Heat oil in a pan and sauté candlenuts, ginger and turmeric lightly.
- Add vinegar, water and salt. Bring to the boil, then simmer for 10–15 minutes.
- Pour cooked liquid over onions. Leave to cool, then cover and let stand for at least 3 days before serving.

Opposite: Acar Buncis

Rujak Buah-buah Pedes

(Hot Fruit Chutney)

Ingredients

Tart apples or green mangoes	2, or ½ yam bean (jicama)
Hard, green pears	2
Sugar	1 tsp
Sweet soy sauce (*kecap manis*)	1 tsp
Tamarind (*asam Jawa*) juice (see pg 16)	1 Tbsp
Sambal oelek (see pg 159)	1 tsp

Method

- Peel fruit and cut into medium-thick slices. Set aside.
- Mix sugar, soy sauce, tamarind juice and *sambal oelek* together in a bowl.
- Add in fruit and stir thoroughly. Serve.

Acar Campur

(Mixed Pickles)

Ingredients

Cabbage	225 g (7½ oz), sliced into strips
String beans	225 g (7½ oz), sliced into strips
Carrot	1, peeled if desired and sliced into strips
Turmeric (*kunyit*)	1 tsp, ground
Sugar	1½ Tbsp
Vinegar	85 ml (⅓ cup)
Water	165 ml (⅔ cup)
Salt	2 tsp

Method

- Parboil all sliced vegetables and drain. Set aside.
- In a clean saucepan, bring turmeric, sugar, vinegar, water and salt to the boil. Pour cooked liquid over mixed vegetables.
- Cover and let stand for at least 6 hours before serving.

Opposite: Acar Campur (top); Rujak Buah-buah Pedes (bottom)

Acar Campur Oelek 〜

(Spicy Mixed Pickles)

Ingredients

Onion	1, medium, peeled
Sambal oelek (see pg 123)	1 tsp
Candlenuts (*kemiri*)	2, grated
Vegetable oil	2 Tbsp
Water	125 ml (½ cup)
Vinegar	85 ml (⅓ cup)
Salt	⅔ tsp
Cabbage	½ head, finely chopped, about 2 cups should result
String beans	225 g (8 oz), finely chopped
Carrot	1, peeled if desired and finely chopped

Method

- Sauté onion, *sambal oelek* and candlenuts in vegetable oil. Then, add water, vinegar and salt. Bring to a slow boil.
- Add in vegetables and cook until tender. Cool, then serve.

Rujak Sayur Pedes 〜

(Spicy Vegetable Chutney)

Ingredients

Sweet soy sauce (*kecap manis*)	1 tsp
Vinegar	2 Tbsp
Salt	½ tsp
Brown sugar	2 tsp
Sambal oelek (see pg 159)	1 tsp
Dried prawn (shrimp) paste (*terasi*)	1 pea-size piece
Firm tomatoes	2, peeled and quartered
Cucumber	1, small, peeled and diced
Radishes	2, sliced

Method

- Mix soy sauce, vinegar, salt, brown sugar, *sambal oelek* and dried prawn paste together.
- Add vegetables and stir well. Serve.

Opposite: Rujak Sayur Pedes

Desserts and Drinks

Indonesian buffet luncheons or dinners, that is, *rijsttafel*, invariably end with a bowl of fresh fruit. Little wonder: there simply is no place for rich desserts. This is not to suggest that the islanders do not like sweets. Indonesians usually restrict their intake of rich, glazed cakes to either festive occasions or coffee-tea breaks.

Sometimes a *rijsttafel* is concluded with bananas lightly fried in coconut oil or margarine, or perhaps a rice-flour pancake filled with grated coconut and palm sugar or caramelised sugar. The fried banana is often served with the rice table itself. In the big Indonesian seaports and towns, such Western concoctions as ice cream or sherbets are also popular desserts.

Perhaps the principal reason why Indonesians place such emphasis on fresh fruits is their natural abundance on most of the islands. Their variety is staggering, even when compared to the rest of Southeast Asia. The banana, for example, comes in many varieties. Among the most popular is the *pisang Ambon* or Ambonese banana, which resembles the Central American variety found in European and North American supermarkets. There is also the *pisang batu* or stone banana which is pitted with tiny, granite-like seeds or stones. The lady-finger banana (also called gold banana or *pisang emas*), which is, as the name suggests, about the length of a lady's finger, is a delight. By contrast, there is the *pisang panjang* or long banana, which is a foot in length. Perhaps the sweetest to the taste is the *pisang susu* or milk banana. Among the bananas, there is also the *pisang raja*, which as its name implies, is the king of bananas.

Similarly, the islanders do not have one kind of pineapple, papaya or mango, but many varieties. The wide-ranging number of *jeruk* or citrus fruits found in Indonesia is stunning. Indeed, the common grapefruit and many other citrus fruits grown around the world are native to the archipelago. Sometimes the size is startling, if not staggering. The *jeruk Bali* or pomelo is a case in point. It is the size of a coconut. What makes Indonesian fruit spectacular is the fantastic variety (some of which defy description and have no colloquial Western names), such as the mangosteen, rambutan, durian, blimbing, jackfruit, *kedong-dong, sawa, duku-duku, jambu, salak* and so forth. Many of these are found in the marketplaces of Southeast Asia, notably Singapore, Bangkok, Kuala Lumpur and Yangon.

The mangosteen has been universally acclaimed by travellers from China and the West as the "queen of fruits". It has been compared by the Dutch plantologist, Jacobus Bontius, to nectar and ambrosia. It has been said to surpass the taste of the golden apples of the Hesperides. Indeed, one American botanist concluded: "It is doubtful whether the world possesses another tropical fruit which is its equal." Yet on the Indonesian islands, the mangosteen grows wild. It can be found growing in almost every village. The fruit is the size of an apple, has a vivid, purple skin and a translucent pulp of indescribable deliciousness. Mangosteen combines the flavour of the nectarine peach and palm to develop an hypnotic sensation of its own. In season, it is commonly served at the end of a *rijsttafel*.

The second fruit on the list is the rambutan (in Malay, *rambut* means hair). About the size of a lemon, the rambutan is usually red in colour, sometimes greenish-yellow. It is covered with ugly, unappetising hairs but the shell is soft and can be easily split to expose a juicy, acidulous, white mass. Probably the closest fruit to rambutan is the Chinese lychee (litchi). The first Westerner who stumbled on the rambutan was a Frenchman who immediately dubbed it *litchi chevelu* — the hairy lychee.

Lychees, incidentally, make an excellent climax to a *rijsttafel* and can be obtained these days as easily in England or Australia as anywhere else. They are invariably tinned in China, Taiwan or Hong Kong. Writing about lychee always vividly brings to mind the finest I have ever eaten. It was in 1949, when my husband and I joined Chokorda, Agung Gede Agung Sukawati in Ubud, Bali, under a lychee tree. We spent the better part of the day leaning against the tree, chatting aimlessly and munching on the fresh fruit swinging gently above our heads. After two or three hours, a small European car flashed by the village and the Chokorda seemed troubled. "Bali is becoming so hasty," he sighed. The last time I saw the Chokorda at Ubud was in 1954. By then, tourism had regained some of its pre-war lustre and I counted eight cars passing through in a single day. The din was dreadful.

No commentary on Indonesia's fruit is complete without reference to the controversial durian. Nature has provided the durian with greater protection than that possibly enjoyed by any other fruit. Its outer skin is spiked and it gives off a rancid, putrid, vile, disagreeable, incredibly bad odour. As for its pulp, however, either you like it or you do not. Unlike the olive, a taste for it cannot be acquired (The best durian I have ever eaten were on the island of Borneo). In 1599, a European traveller in Java noted that "The durian is about the size of a pineapple. Its pulp is like mellow custard." Since then many writers have attempted to describe its taste. For Alfred Russel Wallace who, with Charles Darwin, shares the theory on the origin of species and whose monumental work, *The Malay Archipelago*, is a treasure-trove of information about the islands, the durian tastes like "rich, butter-like custard highly flavoured with almonds". This, he confessed, only gives a general idea of its taste. "But intermingled with it comes wafts of flavour that call to mind cream cheese, onion sauce, brown sherry and other incongruities," he said. "It is neither acid or sweet, nor juicy, yet one feels the want of none of these qualities for it is perfect as it is. In fact, to eat durian is a new sensation, worth a voyage to the East to experience."

These few paragraphs provide only a hint of the variety of fruit found in the Indonesian archipelago, indeed, in the Malay world. It also explains why the *rijsttafel* often ends on a fruity note. The suggestion, then, is that you end your rice table or buffet with a basket of fruit. Use whatever is at hand, whether tropical or cold-weather fruits such as cherries, pears, apples, grapes and so forth.

Pisang Goreng ✦

(Banana Fritters)

Ingredients

Eggs	2
Plain (all-purpose) flour	6 Tbsp
Water	125 ml (½ cup)
Ripe bananas	2
Cooking oil for deep-frying	
Cinnamon sugar	

Method

- Lightly beat eggs and mix with flour and water.
- Separately mash bananas with a fork and mix thoroughly with flour-and-egg mixture.
- Deep-fry banana batter by the tablespoonful in hot oil until golden brown.
- Drain on absorbent paper towels and dust with cinnamon sugar.

NOTE: If you use thinly sliced pineapple instead of mashed banana, you come up with Nanas Goreng (Pineapple Fritters).

Buah-buah Amandel ✦

(Almond Delight)

Ingredients

Milk	250 ml (1 cup)
Water	250 ml (1 cup)
Sugar	4 Tbsp
Unflavoured gelatin	1 envelope (9 g), or sufficient agar-agar to get 500 ml (2 cups) liquid
Almond essence (extract)	1 Tbsp or more to taste
Canned fruit	1 can (312 g), use lychee (litchi), mandarin orange, rambutan or fruit cocktail

Method

- In a small pot, bring milk, water and sugar to a rapid boil. Turn off heat. With a fork, beat unflavoured gelatin into the mixture. Pour cooked mixture into a dish. Allow to stand and cool slightly.
- Add almond essence and mix well. Cover and refrigerate overnight.
- To serve, pour your choice of canned fruit over almond jelly, including the soaking syrup. Although any kind of fruit can be used, mandarin orange goes well as the snowy white and orange make a lovely combination.

Opposite: Buah-buah Amandel

Soursop Gelatin Dessert ⤫

In this recipe, I have used a can of soursop nectar, readily available in most supermarkets.

Ingredients

Soursop nectar	1 can (360 ml) or more to taste
Sugar	1 Tbsp
Unflavoured gelatin	1 envelope (9 g), or sufficient agar-agar to thicken water

Method

- Pour nectar into a large measuring cup and add sufficient water to make 500 ml (2 cups) of liquid.
- In a small pot, mix all ingredients together and, stirring constantly, bring to a simmer.
- Pour this mixture into a dish and allow to return to room temperature.
- Cover tightly and refrigerate for several hours until firm.
- Cut chilled gelatin into cubes and serve. If desired, add some additional soursop nectar.

NOTE: With its large population of Latin Americans and West Indians, soursop is readily available under the Spanish name of *guanabana*. The Dutch name is *zuurzak* and the Latin name is *annona muricata*. You can use this recipe with other types of nectars and serve a gelatin mix.

Lemet ⤫

Ingredients

Tapioca (cassava)	1, grated, about 200 g (2 cups)
Coconut	about 150 g (1½ cups), grated
Sugar	180 g (¾ cup)
Cinnamon	1 tsp, ground
Vanilla essence (extract)	1 tsp
Banana leaves for wrapping	
Bamboo toothpicks or cocktail sticks	

Method

- In a large bowl, combine tapioca, coconut, sugar, cinnamon and vanilla essence. Mix well and set aside.
- Cut banana leaves into rectangles, each 22.5 x 17.5 cm (9 x 7 inches).
- Spoon 1 Tbsp prepared mixture onto the centre of a leaf. Fold leaf over to flatten and shape mixture into a 10-cm length; it should look like a flat sausage.
- Wrap leaf around mixture and fold in ends; the wrapped packet should completely encompass the mixture. Secure folded ends with bamboo toothpicks or cocktail sticks.
- Repeat wrapping process until ingredients are used up. About 24 packets should result.
- When done wrapping, place packets into a large, covered pot and boil for 1 hour 30 minutes. Drain before serving.

NOTE: *Lemet* can be eaten warm or at room temperature. You can also store them in the refrigerator and reheat banana-leaf covered *lemet* in a microwave oven. You can use aluminium foil if banana leaves are unavailable. Foil is easier to fold but the banana leaf imparts a distinct flavour to the *lemet*.

Tropical Fruit Granita ∽

A refreshing finish to a meal, this recipe for granita can be easily applied to a variety of tropical fruit pulps, such as mango, guava and pineapple. I have used soursop as the example in the recipe because I like the combination of sweet and sour.

Ingredients

Frozen soursop pulp	1 package (360 g / 12 oz)
Sugar	180 g (¾ cup)
Water	125 ml (½ cup)

Method

- Thaw frozen fruit pulp, then transfer to a medium-size bowl. You should have about 1½ cups of pulp.
- In a small saucepan, combine sugar and water. Heat until sugar is dissolved.
- Add sugar syrup to fruit pulp in bowl and stir until well mixed.
- Transfer fruit-syrup mixture to a 20-cm (8-inch) square pan and place in the freezer.
- With a fork, scrape the granita every half hour. You do not want a solid, but a granular ice.

Rose Syrup ∽

Ingredients

Water	500 ml (2 cups)
Sugar	480 g (2 cups)
Rose essence (extract)	1 tsp
Red food colouring (optional)	2 drops

Method

- Bring water and sugar to the boil in a large pot, then remove from heat and leave to cool.
- Add rose essence and food colouring, if desired.

NOTE: This syrup can be kept in a tightly sealed bottle in the refrigerator for months.

Ginger Syrup ∽

Ginger syrup is a staple in our home. We pour it in soda water (club soda) for a refreshing drink, put it in our hot tea and drizzle it over pancakes or vanilla ice cream. When I was growing up, making this syrup was time-consuming because we did not have blenders (processors) at home. Now, it's easy and fast to make.

Ingredients

Fresh ginger	675 g (1 lb 7½ oz), peeled
Water	1.5 litres (6 cups)
Citric acid	1 tsp, or juice of 1 lemon
Sugar	

Method

- Cut peeled ginger into small pieces, roughly 2.5-cm (1-inch) lengths. About 2 cups of clean ginger should result.
- Put ginger into a large bowl and add 500 ml (2 cups) water.
- In small batches, transfer ginger and equal amounts of water to blender (processor) and blend until fine.
- Transfer blended ginger to a large pot and add remaining water. Bring to the boil, then reduce heat and simmer for 20 minutes.
- Remove pot from heat and leave to cool. Allow to stand for at least 6 hours or overnight.
- Strain ginger solution through several layers of cheesecloth or a fine sieve. If necessary, strain solution more than once; there should be no bits of ginger in the liquid.
- For every 250 ml (1 cup) of ginger liquid, add 240 g (1 cup) sugar. Then, cook over medium heat until thickened, about 45 minutes. Stir occasionally.
- Remove from heat and add citric acid (or lemon juice) and stir well. Skim off any foam. Leave to cool slightly, then pour into glass bottles.
- Refrigerated syrup can last for months. If syrup thickens too much in refrigerator, return liquid to room temperature before use.

Es Kelapa
(Iced Coconut)

This is a cool, refreshing drink with coconut and crushed ice, and a year-round drink in the tropics. Vendors sell these coconut-based, iced drinks with different flavoured syrups. The version here is a basic one containing our favourite syrup — rose.

Ingredients
Crushed ice	
Milk	125 ml (½ cup)
Flesh of young coconut	
Rose syrup (see pg 179)	1 tsp

Method
- In a blender (processor), mix all ingredients together on high speed.

NOTE: In the West, cans of young coconut flesh can be bought. Simply make sure that the can says "young" and "unsweetened".

Fried Bananas Flambé

Ingredients
Bananas

Margarine

Cointreau, Grand Marnier, rum or cognac

Method
- Peel bananas and sauté them whole in a non-stick pan in margarine.
- Transfer cooked bananas to a serving dish.
- To serve, pour over a few Tbsp of alcohol of choice and light a match. Watch the blue flame flicker away — a truly spectacular sight, and the end-product tastes great as well.

NOTE: In the United States and Europe, large bananas are likely to be available. Peel them and slice in half before sautéing.

Serikaya
(Coconut Custard)

Ingredients
Eggs	4
Sugar	6 Tbsp
Coconut milk	500 ml (2 cups), squeezed from 1 grated coconut with sufficient water added

Brown sugar or palm sugar (*gula Jawa*)

Method
- Beat eggs and sugar together until sugar is dissolved. Mix with coconut milk. Set aside.
- Line individual cups (Pyrex, for instance) with a bit of brown sugar or a piece of brown sugar. Pour coconut mixture into cups until full.
- Onto a steaming rack in pan of water, put filled cups and steam until cooked, about 30–40 minutes. Test with a toothpick or knife in the centre. If it comes out clean, the custard is done.
- Remove cooked custard and allow to cool, then refrigerate.
- Before serving dip a knife in hot water and loosen the edges. Place a serving dish on top and turn out coconut custard; it should pop right out.

NOTE: This dish can also be made in a single large pie dish.

Opposite: Serikaya

Glossary of Ingredients

Asian Aubergine or Eggplant

In South and Southeast Asia, this elongated variety of the aubergine or eggplant is better known as brinjal. Its shape aside, the brinjal is no different from its stubbier but similarly coloured relative, reducing to a pasty texture with prolonged cooking. The Thai aubergine or eggplant is another Asian variety. It is usually speckled white and green and about the size of a golf ball. It, too, has a similar taste and texture when cooked.

Lemon Grass

Lemon grass imparts a delicate but distinct lemon-like fragrance. Whether fresh or frozen, use only the bulbous end, about 12.5 cm (5 inches) from the bottom. With each stalk, cut off the end and leafy top section, then bruise with the back of a knife to release its fragrance before adding to other ingredients to cook. Alternative preparation usually involves mincing because lemon grass is extremely fibrous. Lemon grass is also available ground or in a powdered form.

Salam leaves

Salam leaves are often misidentified as Indonesian or Indian bay leaves by suppliers. *Salam* leaves are not part of the botanical family that includes bay leaves, and are often used to flavour liquid-based dishes. If unavailable fresh or dried, then omit altogether because its flavour, while subtle, is inimitable.

Fermented Soy Bean Cakes

Popularly known as *tempe*, these cakes of skinned soy beans make tasty and inexpensive nourishment. Cakes of *tempe* are usually cut up and browned in oil before they are worked into a dish. In Asia, ready-made *tempe* is sold wrapped in leaves.

Palm Sugar

In Southeast Asia, palm sugar tends to take the form of hard cylindrical pieces slightly smaller than a 300-ml (10-fl. oz) canned drink. They are called *gula Jawa* in Indonesia and *gula Melaka* in Singapore and Malaysia. A slightly different variety, jaggery or *gur*, is common in India. Palm sugar generally is made by cooking and reducing the sap of certain, usually native, palms and so varies slightly from place to place, depending on the species of the plant. The cylindrical shapes imply that the cooked palm sugar syrup was poured into segments of bamboo to harden.

Kaffir Lime Leaves

Also called double lime leaves, kaffir lime leaves are very flavourful, especially when shredded. For a less pungent effect, either bruise or roughly tear them before adding to a dish. Kaffir lime leaves are usually available fresh or frozen, and sometimes come still attached to short lengths of branches, which have sharp thorns. Kitchen scissors are recommended for separating the leaves from their branches. The kaffir lime itself is about the size of a golf ball and has intensely knobby skin, which led to its unflattering colloquial Cantonese name of "leprous lime". The lime has a very thick peel and gives little juice.

Chillies or Hot Peppers

What North Americans call hot peppers, Asians generally know as chillies. The rule of thumb here is that the smaller the chilli, whether red or green, the hotter or more fiery its taste. Rarely exceeding 5 cm (2 inches) in length, the bird's eye chilli, or *cili padi* in Malay, is a case in point. Another handy point to remember is that most of the chilli's fieriness is in its seeds. Deseed it and its potency dips considerably. Alternatively, use the chillies whole.

Tamarind pulp

Known to Indonesians as *asam Jawa*, tamarind pulp is sour-tasting and sold in blocks containing a lot of hard, dark brown seeds. A recipe usually calls for tamarind juice, which is derived by stirring an amount of pulp in some warm water and then straining that mixture. If a more tangy taste is preferred, make a more concentrated juice and vice versa. When a recipe calls for a quantity of just tamarind pulp, be mindful to remove the seeds, bits of broken pod and fibres first.

Dried Sour Fruit

These gnarled, brownish slices are called *asam gelugur* in both Bahasa Indonesia and Malaysia but have no name in English as yet. "Dried sour fruit" is a direct translation of *asam gelugur*. Many suppliers misidentify these dried slices as tamarind skins or slices even though they are botanically unrelated to tamarind. They do, however, serve a similar function of imparting a tangy taste, but one tarter than tamarind. Dried sour fruit slices are usually added to liquid-based dishes and the longer they are cooked, the more sour the dish becomes. Remove and discard the slices when the desired sourness has been achieved.

Shallots

In much of Asian cookery, shallots, and garlic for that matter, are often peeled, sliced and crisp-fried to become a flavoursome garnish. When eaten raw, these small, purple bulbs have a more concentrated taste than larger, white onions. If shallots are unavailable, substitute with the onions at hand, although crisps made from larger onions will not be as deeply aromatic and tasty as crisp-fried shallots.

Weights and Measures

Quantities for this book are given in Metric and American (spoon and cup) measures. Standard spoon and cup measurements used are: 1 tsp = 5 ml, 1 Tbsp = 15 ml, 1 cup = 250 ml. All measures are level unless otherwise stated.

LIQUID AND VOLUME MEASURES

Metric	Imperial	American
5 ml	$^1/_6$ fl oz	1 teaspoon
10 ml	$^1/_3$ fl oz	1 dessertspoon
15 ml	$^1/_2$ fl oz	1 tablespoon
60 ml	2 fl oz	$^1/_4$ cup (4 tablespoons)
85 ml	$2^1/_2$ fl oz	$^1/_3$ cup
90 ml	3 fl oz	$^3/_8$ cup (6 tablespoons)
125 ml	4 fl oz	$^1/_2$ cup
180 ml	6 fl oz	$^3/_4$ cup
250 ml	8 fl oz	1 cup
300 ml	10 fl oz ($^1/_2$ pint)	$1^1/_4$ cups
375 ml	12 fl oz	$1^1/_2$ cups
435 ml	14 fl oz	$1^3/_4$ cups
500 ml	16 fl oz	2 cups
625 ml	20 fl oz (1 pint)	$2^1/_2$ cups
750 ml	24 fl oz ($1^1/_5$ pints)	3 cups
1 litre	32 fl oz ($1^3/_5$ pints)	4 cups
1.25 litres	40 fl oz (2 pints)	5 cups
1.5 litres	48 fl oz ($2^2/_5$ pints)	6 cups
2.5 litres	80 fl oz (4 pints)	10 cups

OVEN TEMPERATURE

Regulo	°C	°F	Gas
Very slow	120	250	1
Slow	150	300	2
Moderately slow	160	325	3
Moderate	180	350	4
Moderately hot	190/200	370/400	5/6
Hot	210/220	410/440	6/7
Very hot	230	450	8
Super hot	250/290	475/550	9/10

DRY MEASURES

Metric	Imperial
30 grams	1 ounce
45 grams	$1^1/_2$ ounces
55 grams	2 ounces
70 grams	$2^1/_2$ ounces
85 grams	3 ounces
100 grams	$3^1/_2$ ounces
110 grams	4 ounces
125 grams	$4^1/_2$ ounces
140 grams	5 ounces
280 grams	10 ounces
450 grams	16 ounces (1 pound)
500 grams	1 pound, $1^1/_2$ ounces
700 grams	$1^1/_2$ pounds
800 grams	$1^3/_4$ pounds
1 kilogram	2 pounds, 3 ounces
1.5 kilograms	3 pounds, $4^1/_2$ ounces
2 kilograms	4 pounds, 6 ounces

LENGTH

Metric	Imperial
0.5 cm	$^1/_4$ inch
1 cm	$^1/_2$ inch
1.5 cm	$^3/_4$ inch
2.5 cm	1 inch

ABBREVIATION

tsp	teaspoon
Tbsp	tablespoon
g	gram
kg	kilogram
ml	millilitre